On Time

Re-examining the End Times and Jesus' Return

By Jon Paul Miles

Edited by Karen Rogers

Amazon Paperback ISBN: 979-8-3753-0243-0

Amazon Hardcover ISBN: 979-8-3773-0097-7

Barnes & Noble Press Paperback ISBN: 979-8-3692-2016-0

Barnes & Noble Press Hardcover ISBN: 979-8-3692-2019-1

Edited by Karen Rogers.

Book Cover Background Image Credits: James Tissot (French, 1836-1902). Jesus Discourses with His Disciples (Jésus s'entretient avec ses disciples), 1886-1896. Opaque watercolor over graphite on gray wove paper, Image: 6 13/16 x 11 11/16 in. (17.3 x 29.7 cm). Brooklyn Museum, Purchased by public subscription, 00.159.165 (Photo: Brooklyn Museum, 00.159.165_PS2.jpg)

Table of Contents

Acknowledgements

There are several individuals whom I would like to acknowledge for helping me throughout this process; they have given me encouragement, guidance, and sometimes even material from their own work to make this book complete. I would like to thank:

- My Lord and Savior Jesus Christ for opening my eyes to the scriptures even when I was at first resistant to him in this matter. He graciously cared for me and gave me the courage to write. This work is only possible because of him.
- My amazing wife, Gabby Miles, who continually shows her love and support and was the first to suggest I write a book. She gave me the confidence that I could write one.
- My editor, Karen Rogers, who dedicated dozens of hours editing my book and offered keen insights, edits, and suggestions to make this book more clear and easy to understand. Her love for the Lord, love of her craft, and support for my work erased my reservations to release this book.
- Dedicated researcher, Daniel Morais, who kindly answered many questions and allowed me to quote much of his material in my chapters on the beasts of Revelation. His continued research into the historical

fulfillment of Biblical prophecy has been vital to this work.

- A good friend and writer, Robert Cruickshank, who has talked with me about these subjects for hours, answered questions, and even provided some of his pre-manuscript material for use in this book.
- My close friend, Nicholas Hasapaglou, who has been an enthusiastic supporter of my work. He has provided critical insight and advice and also helped me to see my work from the eyes of the reader.
- Scholar and researcher, Edward E. Stevens, for his scholarly research and willingness to answer my questions with grace and for allowing me to use some of his material in this book.
- The many other friends and family who have helped me shape my views, offered their love and support, and conversed with me for hours on these subjects.

This book would not be what it is without these individuals, and I want to express my appreciation to them. I also want to thank you, the reader, for having the courage to pick up such a controversial work and consider it.

My Journey

Hello friends! Thank you for taking the time to read my material and critically think it through. I understand many of the ideas I share may seem novel and difficult to digest. I had many concerns and questions, probably like you, when I first came to this view of the end times. It took much prayer, study, courage, and humility to trust God's word and his guidance that I was not being led astray when accepting such a controversial belief.

I was born and raised Christian. I gave my life to the Lord and accepted him as my Lord and Savior at the age of four, was baptized a few years later, and have continued to live my life close to the Lord in prayer, study, conversation, and trust. My faith in Christ and all he's done for us on the cross is the most encouraging and joyous thing in my life. I am eternally grateful and in awe of his continual love, grace, and once-and-for-all sacrifice for us. I love to share how good God is anytime I get the chance.

I grew up in a non-denominational church and for nineteen years assumed the end times were in our near future. However, around 2009, an elder and scholar from our church, Jared Black, led a fascinating Bible study that explained some of the cultural and historical context for the book of Revelation, noting that when Revelation said "the time is near" (Revelation 1:3) it should be understood at face value. He pointed out that several unique events in the first century seemed to fulfill a few of the prophecies in the book of Revelation. His explanations made a lot of sense and piqued my curiosity to research first century events as fulfillments of Revelation's prophecies. I discovered Herald Eberle with his YouTube series on the end times called "Victorious Eschatology," and I found myself agreeing with the idea that much of Revelation was already fulfilled in the first century.[1] At the time, I discovered other preachers who taught that all of Revelation was fulfilled and we were living in the new heavens and new earth. Their interpretations seemed overly spiritualized and overlooked any literal application of the prophecies in the book of Revelation. After hearing Eberle and others who shared his view warn that the belief that all of Revelation was fulfilled was blasphemous, I too considered it blasphemous. For eight years I remained convinced that we were living sometime in the Millennium but believed that Christ would return in our near future. However, unanswered questions led me to explore the subject again years later. Through prayer and research, I discovered that a more literal, on-time fulfillment of Revelation's prophecies was possible, and I was convinced that Jesus returned in the first century.

I did not come to this unique perspective on the end times without a lot of research, prayer, and reflection; I spent several years testing and confirming if this perspective was true. I was convinced that although a fulfilled view of the end times was controversial, it was true. I have held this position since 2018; however, I am still on this journey, researching and seeking

---

[1] Eberle, Herald. 2011. "Victorious Eschatology - Part I." YouTube. https://www.youtube.com/watch?v=J5xDdkzlmWc.

answers to difficult questions. I remain a Christian, a devoted follower of Christ, and care deeply about my faith.

I hope you ask God to help you understand the end times like I did and then trust where he takes you. Do not believe me just because I have done a lot of study; instead, let the Holy Spirit and the Scriptures be your guide to truth.

The end times are not a matter of salvation and should not be an issue the church needs to divide over. If you do find yourself agreeing with this position, I encourage you to unite with our brothers and sisters in Christ as far as it depends on you because of his finished work for us on the cross. Do not let the impactful but tangential discussion of the end times hinder meaningful relationships. And if you wish to share your new end times perspective, do so in love and patience.

Sincerely, Jon Paul

> 1 Corinthians 13:1-3 (English Standard Version) If I speak in the tongues of men and of angels, but have not love, I am a noisy gong or a clanging cymbal. 2 And if I have prophetic powers, and understand all mysteries and all knowledge, and if I have all faith, so as to remove mountains, but have not love, I am nothing. 3 If I give away all I have, and if I deliver up my body to be burned, but have not love, I gain nothing.

Preface
History Matters

Almost half of Christians in the twenty-first century believe they are living in the end times.[2] It is not unusual to hear Christians speculate that Covid is a sign of the last days.[3] The locusts that swarmed Africa in 2020 were the plagues of Revelation.[4] World events, new leaders, red moons, wars, famines, and dangers are taken as proof that our generation is the last. Jesus said the world will get much worse before the end (Matthew 24:9-13), fueling blind pessimism and paranoia over the future of this world.

In his book *Victorious Eschatology,* Harold Eberle captures the pessimism that most Christians feel about the end times. He writes:

> The futurists teach that in the near future there will be great earthquakes, famines, and wars. Then an antichrist will take over the world by establishing one world government, one economic system, and a false religion. This antichrist will then deceive the mass of humanity into following him and cut off the heads of Christians who will

---

[2] Diamant, Jeff. 2022. "About four-in-ten U.S. adults believe humanity is 'living in the end times.'" Pew Research Center. https://www.pewresearch.org/fact-tank/2022/12/08/about-four.

[3] Dein, Simon. 2020. "Covid-19 and the Apocalypse: Religious and Secular Perspectives." NCBI. https://www.ncbi.nlm.nih.gov/pmc/articles/PMC7598223/.

[4] BBC. 2020. "Hundreds of billions of locusts swarm in East Africa." BBC. https://www.bbc.com/news/in-pictures-51618188.

> not receive his mark. Then God will release His wrath upon the world, burning up one-third of the earth and inflicting great pain upon humanity during a seven-year tribulation. Even more discouraging is the futurist's belief that the Church will experience a great falling away before the tribulation, with masses of people abandoning the true Church. Indeed, God will have the victory in the end, but the road between now and then is devastating according to the futurist view.
>
> ...
>
> The futurist view is deeply intertwined with the belief that this world is getting worse and worse, while at the same time, balancing on the brink of destruction. Jack Van Impe, one of the most popular futurist teachers, warns, "All hell will break loose on planet earth—a furious time of pain, mayhem, and agony for millions," and "the signs of global economic chaos are on the horizon."12 Hal Lindsey starts off his tremendously popular book, *The Late Great Planet Earth*, by telling the reader about the "World in a Mess."13 John Hagee, one of the strongest radio and television personalities promoting the futurist view, writes that the world is "standing on the brink of nuclear Armageddon" and "teetering on the brink of World War III."[5]

Although the majority can manage this stressful viewpoint of the world through their hope of Christ's return and a rapture, others make irrational decisions against their long-term interests. One man moved from the city to the wilderness to

---

[5] Eberle, Harold R., and Martin Trench. 2021. Victorious Eschatology: A Partial Preterist View. Kindle ed. Yakima, Washington: Worldcast Ministries & Publishing.

time in human terms and expects us to take him seriously when he does so.

Soon means soon. God uses “soon” the same way humans do, and he rebuked Israel when they denied the obvious meaning of these words.

Chapter 2
The Timeframe of His Return

If "soon" to God does not mean the "distant future" to humans, when does Jesus promise to return?

> Matthew 16:27-28 (Good News Translation) For the Son of Man is **about to come** in the glory of his Father with his angels, and then he will reward each one according to his deeds. I assure you that **there are some here who will not die** until they have seen the Son of Man come as King.

Jesus said that he was about to come in glory with his angels and the kingdom and judge everyone according to their deeds. He further explained that his return would happen after some, but not all, of those who were listening had died. The transfiguration a few days later (Matthew 17:1-8) could not fulfill this prophecy as is often assumed. None of those listening had passed, there were no angels, and Jesus did not judge everyone according to their deeds. At Pentecost, when the Holy Spirit came upon the disciples (Acts 2), no angels were present, Jesus did not come in glory, the kingdom did not arrive, and no judgment took place. When Peter said Joel's prophecies were happening before their eyes at Pentecost, he made it clear that this prophecy was not the coming of Christ but happened "before the day of the Lord comes, the great and magnificent day" (Acts 2:20 [ESV]). Jesus' prophecy must have occurred sometime after these two events but still within their generation.

Missing "About To?"

Most translations ignore the word "about to" when discussing Christ's return, but it is present in the original Greek as “mellṓ,”[10] meaning “at the very point of acting; ready, ‘about to happen.’”[11]

Below are just a few of many examples where “mellṓ” or its root word variants are used in second coming passages:

> 2 Timothy 4:1 (Literal Standard Version) I fully testify, then, before God, and the Lord Jesus Christ, who is **about to [mellontos]** judge [the] living and dead at His appearing and His Kingdom
>
> Acts 17:31 (Berean Literal Bible) because He set a day in which He is **about to [mellei]** judge the world in righteousness...
>
> Acts 24:15 (LSV) there is **about to [mellein]** be a resurrection of the dead, both of righteous and unrighteous

In his article, "What Will We Do With The Greek Term Mello?" Minister Tony E. Denton says several reputable Greek lexicons and interlinears nearly always (95%) translate “mello” as "about to."[12]

---

[10] “Matthew 16:27 Greek Text Analysis.” n.d. Bible Hub. Accessed December 30, 2022. https://biblehub.com/text/matthew/16-27.htm.

[11] “Strong's Greek: 3195. μέλλω (mellṓ) -- to be about to.” n.d. Bible Hub. Accessed December 30, 2022. https://biblehub.com/greek/3195.htm.

[12] Denton, Tony E. 2008. "What Will We Do With The Greek Term Mello?" A Site For The Lord | Bible Studies And Books. http://asiteforthelord.com/wp-content/uploads/2017/09/MelloByTheScholars1.pdf.

More literal translations of the scriptures will include this phrase, but where its existence may be questioned, BibleHub shows the original Greek of the verse and allows one to confirm if "about to" should be present in the text.

A Soon Return

On other occasions, Jesus indicated he would return soon. While answering the disciples' question about when he would return to destroy the temple and end the age, Jesus told them there would be a Great Tribulation, signs in the stars, and he would return riding on the clouds. After describing all these events, he told them, "this generation will certainly not pass away until all these things have happened." (One can see what was promised in the parallel passages Matthew 24; Mark 13; Luke 17, 21).

> Matthew 24:34 (NIV) Truly I tell you, this generation will certainly not pass away until all these things have happened.

In Luke's account of Jesus' return on the clouds, Jesus told the disciples that these events were "about to happen," helping the reader to interpret the meaning of "this generation."

> Luke 21:35-36 (NIV) For it will come on all those who live on the face of the whole earth. Be always on the watch, and pray that you may be able to escape all that is **about to [mellonta]** happen, and that you may be able to stand before the Son of Man.

Jesus warned the disciples that there would come a time when the world would hate and persecute them. He instructed them to flee from one town to the next, but in case the disciples should worry that every town would reject them, he comforted them with the promise that he would return before they were kicked out of every city.

> Matthew 10:23 (NIV) When you are persecuted in one place, flee to another. Truly I tell you, you will not finish going through the towns of Israel before the Son of Man comes.

While readers often like to place themselves into the text, it is clear in the verse below, that "you" refers specifically to the people speaking to Jesus, and he promised they would live long enough to see him coming on the clouds of heaven.

> Matthew 26:64 (NIV) "**You have said so**," Jesus replied. "**But I say to all of you**: From now on **you will see** the Son of Man sitting at the right hand of the Mighty One and coming on the clouds of heaven."

Jesus intended for the disciple John to live long enough to see his return.

> John 21:21-23 (ESV) When Peter saw him, he said to Jesus, "Lord, what about this man?" 22 Jesus said to him, "If it is my will that he remain until I come, what is that to you? You follow me!" 23 So the saying spread abroad among the brothers that this disciple was not to die; yet Jesus did not say to him that he was not to die, but, "If it is my will that he remain until I come, what is that to you?"

Some Christians wonder if John is still alive today, waiting for Christ's return. However, it makes more sense that John had a normal lifespan and that he lived to see the return of Jesus. Peter, however, would die before Christ came.

Christ would be ashamed of the disciples' generation when he returned because he would return in their generation.

> Mark 8:38 (ESV) For whoever is ashamed of me and of my words in this adulterous and sinful generation, of him will the Son of Man also be ashamed when he comes in the glory of his Father with the holy angels.

The disciples were persecuted for almost forty years by the unbelieving Jews and Gentiles, and Jesus taught that a just judge does not delay in giving justice. Indeed, a delay of two thousand years is unjust. In the scriptures below, Jesus explained it was only just for him to return quickly.

> Luke 18:7-8 (ESV) And will not God give justice to his elect, who cry to him day and night? Will he delay long over them? 8 I tell you, he will give justice to them speedily. Nevertheless, when the Son of Man comes, will he find faith on earth?

Given that God takes time statements seriously and Jesus seemed to promise a tight timeframe for his return, the believer should carefully consider this promise. A biblical generation is forty years (Numbers 32:13), and Jesus promised to return to his generation. Christians frequently offer one of four explanations for Jesus' failed promise to return in his generation.

1. Jesus used false expectations of a near return to motivate perpetual, eager preparedness. Every

generation should believe Jesus is coming in their generation.

2. Jesus did not know when he would come (an interpretation based off Matthew 24:36) and wrongfully assumed the timeframe of his return. C. S. Lewis held this view.[13]

3. God delayed his plans because Israel rejected him, and he worried too many would be lost if he returned on time. This view is argued by Pete Enns, Ph.D.[14] and several verses are used to make this claim (Ezekiel 18:32; 33:11; Matthew 23:39; Acts 3:17-21; 1 Timothy 2:3-4; 2 Peter 3:9).

4. The words of Jesus are misunderstood or mistranslated.

Each of these explanations should be carefully examined to see if they excuse Jesus' words.

The Messiah Cannot Lie

The Messiah cannot lie (Isaiah 53:9; John 12:49-50; 1 Peter 2:22).

> Isaiah 53:9 (ESV) And they made his grave with the wicked and with a rich man in his death, although he had done no violence, and there was no deceit in his mouth.

---

[13] Lewis, World's Last Night, 97-99, https://archive.org/details/worldslastnighta012859mbp/page/n109/mode/2up

[14] Enns, Pete, and Christopher M. Hays. 2016. "When is Jesus Coming Back? Well, The Answer May Shock You." The Bible For Normal People. https://thebiblefornormalpeople.com/on-why-jesus-hasnt-come-back-yet/.

God also commanded his people to judge a prophecy by its promised time frame (Deuteronomy 18:20-22).

> Deuteronomy 18:20-22 (ESV) But the prophet who presumes to speak a word in my name that I have not commanded him to speak, or who speaks in the name of other gods, that same prophet shall die.' 21 And if you say in your heart, 'How may we know the word that the Lord has not spoken?'— 22 when a prophet speaks in the name of the Lord, **if the word does not come to pass or come true**, that is a word that the Lord has not spoken; the prophet has spoken it presumptuously. You need not be afraid of him.

How would anyone know if a prophecy did not come to pass or prove true unless it was judged by time? The Jews were to ignore and kill the prophet if the prophecy did not occur on time, "that same prophet shall die" (Deuteronomy 18:20).

If Jesus wanted to persuade every generation that he could come during their lifetime, Jesus would have told them he could come at any time, not limit himself to one generation. If he wanted to motivate continued preparation, he would not have given a specific timeframe. It is unthinkable for Jesus to lie.

Jesus Was Certain

No honest person uses the language Jesus used to express an assumption, "Truly I tell you, this generation will certainly not pass away until all these things have happened. Heaven and earth will pass away, but my words will never pass away." Only someone certain that what they are saying is true uses such language.

Jesus begins with "Truly I tell you," declaring that what he says is true and beyond doubt. The word "certainly" in the above verse has been translated from the Greek phrase "ou mé,"[15] which is more dramatic. This phrase extra-emphatically and forcefully conveys that something is "not a fact" and "not even a possibility."[16] His words conveyed that it was not even possible that the disciples' generation would pass before everything he prophesied happened.

If Jesus was mistaken, the Holy Spirit of Truth should have cleared up this confusion with the disciples. Otherwise the Spirit would have been complicit in Jesus' misinformation.

> John 16:13 (ESV) When the Spirit of truth comes, he will guide you into all the truth, for he will not speak on his own authority, but whatever he hears he will speak, and he will declare to you the things that are to come.

God Cannot Delay

Though God may change his plans (Jeremiah 18:5-10), he promised to tell the prophets when he did so.

> Amos 3:3-8 (ESV) For the Lord God does nothing without revealing his secret to his servants the prophets.

If God initially promised to return in his generation and changed his mind, he would have told the prophets. However,

---

[15] "Matthew 24:34 Greek Text Analysis." n.d. Bible Hub. Accessed January 25, 2023. https://biblehub.com/text/matthew/24-34.htm.

[16] "Strong's Greek: 3364. οὐ (ou mé) -- anymore, at all, neither, never." n.d. Bible Hub. Accessed January 25, 2023. https://biblehub.com/greek/3364.htm.

in the final letters of the Bible, the plan remained unchanged. The second from the last verse in Revelation reads:

> Revelation 22:20 (ESV) He who testifies to these things says, "Surely I am coming soon." Amen. Come, Lord Jesus!

Some scholars believe that 2 Peter was written chronologically after Revelation. Even in this letter, Peter never said God had decided to delay his plans. Instead, Peter said:

> 2 Peter 1:19; 3:9 (ESV) We also have the prophetic message as something completely reliable, and you will do well to pay attention to it... The Lord is not slow in keeping his promise

Peter's message was not that God had decided to delay his plans but that God had chosen to wait until the very end of the promised timespan, their generation, to save as many as possible.

If God does not say that he will change his plans, his original word stands true. If those words do not pass as promised, the prophet who delivered those words would be considered false, and his life would be in danger. For the sake of those whom God commands to speak on his behalf, he lets it be known when he changes his plans.

Not only did God never say he would delay his plans, but after promising his return within the apostles' generation, he swore not to delay his plans (Luke 21:32-33; Acts 17:31 [Young's Literal Translation]; Hebrews 10:36-37; Revelation 10:6).

> Revelation 10:6 (ESV) and swore by him who lives forever and ever, who created heaven and what is in it, the earth

> and what is in it, and the sea and what is in it, that there would be no more delay

God cannot break his oaths (Leviticus 5:4-5; Numbers 23:19; 30:1-2; Deuteronomy 23:21-23; Joshua 9:3-21; Judges 11:30-31,34-35; 2 Samuel 21:1-2; Psalm 15:1-2,4; 24:4; Hebrews 6:17-18).

> Hebrews 6:17 (ESV) So when God desired to show more convincingly to the heirs of the promise the **unchangeable** character of his purpose, **he guaranteed it with an oath**

When God makes an oath, he shows that the promise is unchangeable. He told the Israelites that delaying their oath is a sin.

> Deuteronomy 23:21-23 (ESV) "If you make a vow to the Lord your God, you shall not delay fulfilling it, for the Lord your God will surely require it of you, and you will be guilty of sin. 22 But if you refrain from vowing, you will not be guilty of sin. 23 You shall be careful to do what has passed your lips, for you have voluntarily vowed to the Lord your God what you have promised with your mouth.

God uses "delay" the way one assumes (Ezekiel 12:21-28). Therefore, waiting two thousand years to return would be a sin. Since God cannot sin, he therefore could not delay his plans.

If God did not delay his plans or lie about the timing, what if he never promised to return soon in the first place?

Was Jesus Misunderstood?

Scholars suggest alternative meanings to Jesus' words in Matthew 24:34.

> Matthew 24:34 (ESV) Truly, I say to you, this generation [genea[17]] will not pass away until all these things take place.

This Generation or This Race

Dr. Norman Geisler, Ph.D., and others argue that "generation" should be translated as "race," meaning this Hebrew, evil, or elect race will not pass before Christ returns.[18] Jesus used this word "generation" in its most natural sense everywhere else (Matthew 1:17; 11:16; 12:39,41,42,45; 16:4; 17:17; Mark 8:12,38; 9:19; 13:30; Luke 1:48,50; 7:31; 9:41; 11:29-32,50-51; 16:8; 17:25; 21:32). The Greek language contains a separate word for race or kind, "genos" as used in 1 Peter 2:9, "you are a chosen **race [genos]**." However, the word used in Matthew 24:34 is "genea," which is always translated as the present living generation throughout the New Testament and never means a kind or species.[19] If Jesus wanted to communicate, "this race" would not pass; he would have used "genos."

---

[17] "Matthew 24:34 Greek Text Analysis." n.d. Bible Hub. Accessed January 9, 2023. https://biblehub.com/text/matthew/24-34.htm.

[18] Geisler, Norman L. n.d. "A Review of Hank Hanegraaff's The Apocalypse Code – NORMAN GEISLER." Norman Geisler. Accessed December 9, 2022. https://normangeisler.com/a-review-of-hanegraaff-apocalypse-code/.

[19] Brother A-aron. 2020. "Partial-Preterism! Approach to the Book of Revelation: Interview with Bruce Gore." YouTube. https://www.youtube.com/watch?v=aRJluO6AVIw.

This or That Generation

Some argue that in the context of end-time prophecies, "this generation" actually refers to a future generation or the generation that witnesses the signs of the end times. According to this interpretation, the generation observing these signs would not pass away until all the prophecies are fulfilled.[20]

However, remember the disciples' question (Matthew 24:2-3; Mark 13:2,4; Luke 21:6-7).

> Mark 13:1-4 (ESV) And as he came out of the temple, one of his disciples said to him, "Look, Teacher, what wonderful stones and what wonderful buildings!" 2 And Jesus said to him, "Do you see these great buildings? There will not be left here one stone upon another that will not be thrown down." 3 And as he sat on the Mount of Olives opposite the temple, Peter and James and John and Andrew asked him privately, 4 "Tell us, when will these things be, and what will be the sign when all these things are about to be accomplished?"

Jesus told them that the temple they were looking and pointing at would fall. If that temple fell in their first-century generation, why would this not be what Jesus meant by "this generation?"

---

[20] Got Questions Ministries. n.d. "What did Jesus mean when He said, "this generation will not pass"?" gotquestions.org. Accessed December 8, 2022. https://www.gotquestions.org/this-generation-not-pass.html; Evidence Unseen. n.d. "(Mt. 24:34) Did Jesus make a false prediction about his second coming?" Evidence Unseen. Accessed December 9, 2022. https://www.evidenceunseen.com/bible-difficulties-2/nt-difficulties/matthew/mt-2434-did-jesus-make-a-false-prediction-about-his-second-coming/.

Daniel Morais, Ph.D., radio broadcaster and founder of Revelation Revolution Foundation, uses historical accounts to show that the disciples' generation did see all the signs of the end times.[21] Peter, Paul, the author of Hebrews, and John said they saw the final signs and were living in the last days and even the last hour (Acts 2:16-17; 1 Corinthians 10:11; Hebrews 1:1-2; Revelation 1:9; 1 John 2:18).

> Acts 2:15-17 (New Living Translation) These people are not drunk, as some of you are assuming. Nine o'clock in the morning is much too early for that. 16 No, **what you see was predicted long ago by the prophet Joel**: 17 '**In the last days**,' God says, 'I will pour out my Spirit upon all people. Your sons and daughters will prophesy. Your young men will see visions, and your old men will dream dreams.

> Hebrews 1:1-2 (ESV) Long ago, at many times and in many ways, God spoke to our fathers by the prophets, 2 **but in these last days** he has spoken to us by his Son, whom he appointed the heir of all things, through whom also he created the world.

> 1 John 2:18 (ESV) Children, **it is the last hour**, and as you have heard that antichrist is coming, so now many antichrists have come. **Therefore we know that it is the last hour**.

According to early church father Eusebius, the first-century Christians rightfully understood that the tribulation would

---

[21] Morais, Daniel. 2017. "Matthew 24 Commentary: THAT Generation Shall Not Pass." Revelation Revolution Foundation. https://www.revelationrevolution.org/matthew-24-commentary-that-generation-shall-not-pass/.

occur in their generation. Because of Jesus' words, they fled the fortified city of Jerusalem to the remote, mountainous town of Pella to save themselves from its destruction (Revelation 12:6,14).[22] Describing this event, Eusebius wrote:

> But the people of the church in Jerusalem had been commanded by a revelation, vouchsafed to approved men there before the war, to leave the city and to dwell in a certain town of Perea called Pella. And when those that believed in Christ had come there from Jerusalem, then, as if the royal city of the Jews and the whole land of Judea were entirely destitute of holy men, the judgment of God at length overtook those who had committed such outrages against Christ and his apostles, and totally destroyed that generation of impious men.[23]

Epiphanius of Salamis, a church father writing in 377 AD, also described the flight to Pella:

> ...after the exodus from Jerusalem when all the disciples went to live in Pella because Christ had told them to leave Jerusalem and to go away since it would undergo a siege. Because of this advice they lived in Perea after having moved to that place, as I said (Epiphanius, Panarion 29,7,7-8).[24]

---

[22] Maarschalk, Adam. 2017. "Did All of the Judean Christians Flee to Pella?" Adam Maarschalk. https://adammaarschalk.com/2017/01/24/did-all-of-the-judean-christians-flee-to-pella/.

[23] Pamphili of Caesarea, Eusebius. n.d. Church History. Translated by Nicene and Post-Nicene Fathers. Accessed Dec. 9, 2022. https://www.historytimeline.org/docs/eusebius/church_history/, 3.5.3, https://www.historytimeline.org/docs/eusebius/church_history/book_03.php.

[24] Wikipedia. 2022. “Flight to Pella.” Wikipedia. https://en.wikipedia.org/wiki/Flight_to_Pella.

Though the fortified city was usually the safest place during a war, the faith that Jesus was prophesying about their generation spared the disciples from its destruction. John even said he was living in the tribulation:

> Revelation 1:9 (ESV) I, John, your brother and **partner in the tribulation** and the kingdom and the patient endurance that are in Jesus, was on the island called Patmos on account of the word of God and the testimony of Jesus.

The inspired disciples can be trusted to interpret the signs they saw rightfully.

To summarize,

- The generation that sees the end times signs will not pass before everything finishes
- Jesus' generation saw the end times signs
- Therefore, Jesus' generation could not have passed until everything was completed.

The Temple Stands at Christ's Return

One can assume that Jesus returned before the temple fell because he promised to return "immediately after the tribulation of those days" (Matthew 24:29-30; Mark 13:24,26; Luke 17:30-31; 19:43-44).

The temple was standing during the days of tribulation because Daniel prophesied that during the days of tribulation the "abomination of desolation" would stand in the temple (Daniel 11:31; 12:1,11; Matthew 24:15-21; Hebrews 9:2).

Two Returns?

What if only part of the Olivet Discourse applies to the first-century but the rest to the distant future? Prominent scholars including avid writer and co-founder of "Pre-Trib Research Center" Dr. Thomas D. Ice, Ph.D.[25] and World Video Bible School, a popular source of Christian edification,[26] teach that Jesus answered two unrelated questions in the same speech. Their theory divides Matthew 24:3 into two segments, as marked below.

> Matthew 24:3 (ESV) As he sat on the Mount of Olives, the disciples came to him privately, saying, "Tell us, **[1]** when will these things be, and **[2]** what will be the sign of your coming and of the end of the age?"

The school says the first part of the question above, "[1] when will these things be," concerns the temple's fall, the Great Tribulation, and Jesus' symbolic return in the first century. Yet, they claim the second part of the question, "[2] what will be the sign of your coming and of the end of the age?" is answered in Matthew 24:36 and following, describing a third coming at an unknown time at the world's end (Matthew 24:36-51; 25:1-13; Mark 13:32-37; Luke 21:34-36).

However, Jesus promised that even the events of the second supposed segment were near.

---

[25] Ice, Thomas D. 2009. "An Interpretation of Matthew 24-25." Article Archives, no. 2 (May). https://digitalcommons.liberty.edu/cgi/viewcontent.cgi?article=1001&context=pretrib_arch.

[26] World Video Bible School (WVBS). 2015. "Premillennialism: A Deeper Study." YouTube. https://youtu.be/e22iIXj0cVY?t=784.

> Luke 21:36 (NIV) Be always on the watch, and pray that you may be able to escape **all that is about to happen**, and that you may be able to stand before the Son of Man.

The passage above is the parallel of Matthew 24:36 and following. The events that were about to happen included the Son of Man or Master's return (Matthew 24:37,39,42,44,46; Mark 13:35), that is to say the school's supposed "third coming" of Christ.

The other two accounts of the Olivet Discourse, told by Mark and Luke, also make dividing the question into two unrelated parts impossible.

> Mark 13:2-4 (ESV) And Jesus said to him, "Do you see these great buildings? There will not be left here one stone upon another that will not be thrown down."
>
> 3 And as he sat on the Mount of Olives opposite the temple, Peter and James and John and Andrew asked him privately, 4 "**Tell us, when will these things be, and what will be the sign when all these things are about to be accomplished?**"
>
> Luke 21:5-7 (ESV) And while some were speaking of the temple, how it was adorned with noble stones and offerings, he said, 6 "As for these things that you see, the days will come when there will not be left here one stone upon another that will not be thrown down." 7 And they asked him, "**Teacher, when will these things be, and what will be the sign when these things are about to take place?**"

Both Mark and Luke's accounts make it clear that the disciples were asking about when the temple would fall and what would be the sign that it was about to fall, not the temple's fall and the end of the world.

Jesus answered that the temple would fall in their generation and they should look for his return on the clouds as a sign it was about to fall.

> Matthew 24:30,32-34 (ESV) **Then will appear in heaven the sign of the Son of Man...** 32 "From the fig tree learn its lesson: as soon as its branch becomes tender and puts out its leaves, you know that summer is near. 33 So also, when you see all these things, you know that he is near, at the very gates. 34 **Truly, I say to you, this generation will not pass away until all these things take place.**

Why They Must Watch

Jesus wanted his disciples to watch for his coming (Mark 13:32-37), but not for their entertainment or so they could quickly get their act together the day they saw him. Jesus said his return would be like the days of Noah when Noah hid in the ark, and the flood swept the rest away (Matthew 24:37-42; Luke 17:26-27). He said it would be like the day Lot fled Sodom before the city burned (Luke 17:24-37). The disciples must carefully watch because they had to be ready to flee Judea to the mountains to save themselves from Jerusalem's destruction (Matthew 24:15-18; Luke 17:30-33; 21:20-22). Otherwise, they would be like Lot's wife who hesitated and turned into a pillar of salt or like those swept away in Noah's flood. The return of Christ was their signal to escape. If he did not show up before the armies encompassed Jerusalem, they would be trapped inside and destroyed along with it.

Luke 17 Prohibits a Division

Luke 17:22-37 makes it impossible to divide the Olivet Discourse into two sections and therefore two separate returns of Christ (the first being verses Matthew 24:17-36, and the second being Matthew 24:36-25:46). Luke reorders identical statements from the second segment (about the unexpected Son of Man or Master's return) with the first segment (the days of tribulation) and statements from the first segment with the second segment.

The Berean Bible Church of Virginia Beach illustrates why segmenting the Olivet Discourse is impossible:

> Those who attempt to divide Matthew 24 say that SECTION ONE refers to the events of AD 70. But they say SECTION TWO refers to events yet future to us. If the five prophetic events of Matthew 24 that are found in Luke 17 are numbered 1-2-3-4-5, Luke's numbering of the same events would be 2-4-1-5-3. Luke has an event from section 1 followed by one from section 2, then another from section 1 followed by section 2, and finally one from section 1. This shows the impossibility of dividing Matthew 24 with a 2,000 year gap.[27]

---

[27] Berean Bible Church. n.d. "THE OLIVET DISCOURSE CANNOT BE DIVIDED Chart." Berean Bible Church. Accessed December 9, 2022. https://www.bereanbiblechurch.org/transcripts/mark/13_32-37_chart.htm.

Matthew 24

Section 1 (v1-35)

1. 17 Let him who is on the housetop not go down to take out the things that are in his house. 18 Let him who is in the field not return back to get his clothes.

2. 26 "If therefore they tell you, 'Behold, he is in the wilderness,' don't go out; or 'Behold, he is in the inner rooms,' don't believe it. 27 For as the lightning flashes from the east, and is seen even to the west, so will the coming of the Son of Man be.

3. 28 For wherever the carcass is, that is where the vultures gather together.

Section 2 (v36-51)

4. 37 As the days of Noah were, so will the coming of the Son of Man be. 38 For as in those days which were before the flood they were eating and drinking, marrying and giving in marriage, until the day that Noah entered into the ship, 39 and they didn't know until the flood came and took them all away, so will the coming of the Son of Man be.

5. 40 Then two men will be in the field: one will be taken and one will be left. 41 Two women will be grinding at the mill: one will be taken and one will be left.

Luke 17

2. 23 They will tell you, 'Look, here!' or 'Look, there!' Don't go away or follow after them, 24 for as the lightning, when it flashes out of one part under the sky, shines to another part under the sky; so will the Son of Man be in his day.

4. 26 As it was in the days of Noah, even so it will also be in the days of the Son of Man. 27 They ate, they drank, they married, and they were given in marriage until the day that Noah entered into the ship, and the flood came and destroyed them all.

1. 31 In that day, he who will be on the housetop and his goods in the house, let him not go down to take them away. Let him who is in the field likewise not turn back.

5. 35 There will be two grinding grain together. One will be taken and the other will be left."

3. 37 They, answering, asked him, "Where, Lord?" He said to them, "Where the body is, there the vultures will also be gathered together."

World English Bible

Dual Fulfillment

Several scholars believe some Old Testament prophecies have dual fulfillments. Could Jesus' prophecy have a dual fulfillment?

Unfortunately, there is no indication in Jesus' promises that he also implied a second fulfillment. He explicitly stated that the Great Tribulation would never occur again.

> Matthew 24:21 (NIV) For then there will be great distress, unequaled from the beginning of the world until now—**and never to be equaled again**.

If the world would never be in such distress again, then Jesus had one fulfillment in mind.

Jesus Was Understood

Notice that Jesus emphasized his promise precisely because he wanted it to be understood and trusted. "Truly I tell you, this generation will certainly not pass away..." Jesus would select the most unambiguous language to communicate this. After showing his intentions to be understood by the disciples (Luke 8:10), he sent the Holy Spirit in case anything was misunderstood (John 16:13). Therefore, the most reliable way to verify what Jesus promised is to note how his disciples understood him.

What the Disciples Thought

After Jesus rose to heaven, the disciples wrote to the first century believers. They explicitly and repeatedly told Christians that his coming was near (see "Chapter 3 Scriptures of a Soon Return") because they heard Jesus say precisely this. The argument that something allusive was meant by their words "near," "about to come," "have come," "will not delay," "is at hand," "is the last hour," and "the time is near" does not make good sense. By their actions, the disciples proved they expected his soon return.

Actions Speak

The disciples acted in a way that showed they expected the return of Jesus in their lifetime.

- They did not get drunk because they did not want to be caught off guard by Christ's arrival (1 Thessalonians 5:1-8).
- They would meet together more and more frequently as they saw the day approaching (Hebrews 10:25).
- They commanded Christians to be prepared for swift action (1 Peter 1:13).
- They encouraged those afflicted that Jesus would return and give them relief from their persecutors (2 Thessalonians 1:6-7).
- They did not make long-term investments in the world because they expected its current form to end soon (1 Corinthians 7:29-31).

> 1 Corinthians 7:29-31 (ESV) This is what I mean, brothers: the appointed time has grown very short. From now on, let those who have wives live as though

they had none, 30 and those who mourn as though they were not mourning, and those who rejoice as though they were not rejoicing, and those who buy as though they had no goods, 31 and those who deal with the world as though they had no dealings with it. For the present form of this world is passing away.

- They avoided marriage to live more comfortably with the end coming (1 Corinthians 7:26).
- They avoided taking the rich to court for their crimes since they would soon receive justice from God (James 5:9).
- As their generation was about to expire, there was concern that Christ's coming appeared to be delayed (2 Peter 3:4,8-9). The early Christians would not be concerned about a delay if they did not expect his return in their generation.

As shown, the disciples did not merely say Jesus was going to return soon; they acted in the belief that they were about to experience his arrival.

Summary

Conclusively,

- Jesus cannot give false expectations or tell a false prophecy if he is the Messiah.
- No honest person uses the language Jesus used to express an assumption.

- Although God can withdraw a threat or blessing, he does not change his plans when making an oath, and he made an oath to return without delay in that generation and in a "very little while."
- By their words and actions, the disciples demonstrated that they understood Jesus to mean that their generation would not pass before he returned. Jesus did not intend for his disciples to misunderstand him and even sent the Holy Spirit to show them the things that were to come.

No answer except one adequately explains Jesus' words: Jesus promised to return before their generation passed. Hence, to say he did not return as promised calls into question if he was the Messiah and the prophecy itself.

We should not make the same mistake as the Pharisees. The Pharisees rejected Jesus' first coming because he did not come in the way they expected.[28] What if we as believers are rejecting his second coming in the same way the Pharisees rejected his first? Peter tells Christians to be ready to defend the gospel (1 Peter 3:15). Therefore, we should carefully consider how Christ fulfilled the promise of his coming in their generation.

---

[28] Lucey, Candice. 2021. "Why Was the Messiah Expected to Free Israel from Rome?" Christianity. https://www.christianity.com/wiki/jesus-christ/why-was-the-messiah-expected-to-free-israel-from-rome.html.

Chapter 3
Scriptures of a Soon Return

The following are some of the many scriptures written to the first century church, substantiating the promise of a soon return of Jesus.

> Acts 2:15-17 (NLT) These people are not drunk, as some of you are assuming. Nine o'clock in the morning is much too early for that. 16 No, **what you see was predicted long ago by the prophet Joel: 17 'In the last days,'** God says, 'I will pour out my Spirit upon all people. Your sons and daughters will prophesy. Your young men will see visions, and your old men will dream dreams.

> Acts 17:31 (BLB) because He set a day in which He is about to judge the world in righteousness...

> Acts 24:15 (LSV) there is about to be a resurrection of the dead, both of righteous and unrighteous

> Acts 24:25 (LSV) and he reasoning concerning righteousness, and self-control, and the judgment that is about to be

> Romans 4:23-24 (LSV) And it was not written on [Abraham's] his account alone that it [faith] was reckoned to him [as righteousness], but also on ours, to whom it is about to be reckoned

> Romans 8:13 (LSV) for if according to the flesh you live, you are about to die

Romans 8:18 (LSV) For I reckon that the sufferings of the present time [are] not worthy [to be compared] with the glory about to be revealed in us

Romans 9:28 (ESV) for the Lord will carry out his sentence upon the earth fully and without delay.

Romans 13:11-12 (ESV) the hour has come for you to wake from sleep. For salvation is nearer to us now than when we first believed. 12 The night is far gone; the day is at hand.

Romans 16:20 (ESV) The God of peace will soon crush Satan under your feet.

1 Corinthians 7:29 (ESV) the appointed time has grown very short

1 Corinthians 7:31 (ESV) For the present form of this world is passing away.

1 Corinthians 10:11 (ESV) Now these things happened to them as an example, but they were written down for our instruction, on whom the end of the ages has come.

1 Corinthians 15:51-52 (ESV) We shall not all sleep, but we shall all be changed, in a moment, in the twinkling of an eye, at the last trumpet. For the trumpet will sound, and the dead will be raised imperishable, and we shall be changed.

1 Corinthians 16:22 (BLB) "Maranatha!" [The Lord comes!]

Ephesians 1:21 (David Bentley Hart) Far above every Rule and Authority and Power and Lordship, and every name being named not only in this age, but in that about to come;

Philippians 4:5 (ESV) The Lord is at hand.

Colossians 1:23 (ESV) the gospel that you heard, which has been proclaimed in all creation under heaven (Compare

Matthew 24:14; Romans 10:18; 16:26; Colossians 1:5-6; 2 Timothy 4:17; Revelation 14:6-7; cf. 1 Clement 5,7)

Colossians 2:17 (Julia Smith Translation) Which are a shadow of things about to be; and the body of Christ.

1 Thessalonians 4:15,17; 5:4 (ESV) ...we who are alive, who are left until the coming of the Lord... ...we who are alive, who are left, will be caught up together with them in the clouds to meet the Lord in the air... ...But you are not in darkness, brothers, for that day to surprise you like a thief.

1 Thessalonians 5:23 (BLB) may your entire spirit, soul, and body be kept blameless at the coming of our Lord Jesus Christ.

2 Thessalonians 1:6-7 (ESV) since indeed God considers it just to repay with affliction those who afflict you, 7 and to grant relief to you who are afflicted as well as to us, when the Lord Jesus is revealed from heaven with his mighty angels

1 Timothy 4:8 (JST) devotion ...having promise of life now, and that about to be.

1 Timothy 6:14 (ESV) to keep the commandment unstained and free from reproach until the appearing of our Lord Jesus Christ

1 Timothy 6:19 (LSV) treasuring up to themselves a right foundation for the time [about (mellon)] to come, that they may lay hold on [that which is] truly life.

2 Timothy 3:1-2,5-6,8-9 (ESV) that in the last days there will come times of difficulty. 2 For people will be lovers of self... Avoid such people. 6 For among them are those who creep into households and capture weak women... these men also

1 Peter 1:20 (NIV) He was chosen before the creation of the world, but was revealed in these last times for your sake.

1 Peter 4:5 (ESV) but they will give account to him who is ready to judge the living and the dead.

1 Peter 4:7 (ESV) The end of all things is at hand; therefore be self-controlled and sober-minded for the sake of your prayers.

1 Peter 4:17 (ESV) For it is time for judgment to begin at the household of God

1 Peter 5:1 (LSV) [as] a fellow-elder, and a witness of the sufferings of the Christ, and a partaker of the glory about to be revealed,

2 Peter 1:19 (ESV) And we have the prophetic word more fully confirmed, to which you will do well to pay attention as to a lamp shining in a dark place, until the day dawns and the morning star rises in your hearts,

2 Peter 2:3 (ESV) Their condemnation from long ago is not idle, and their destruction is not asleep.

2 Peter 3:3,5 (LSV) that there will come scoffers in the last days ...for this they willingly conceal

2 Peter 3:10-12 (ESV) But the day of the Lord will come like a thief, and then the heavens will pass away with a roar, and the heavenly bodies will be burned up and dissolved, and the earth and the works that are done on it will be exposed. 11 Since all these things are thus to be dissolved, what sort of people ought you to be in lives of holiness and godliness, 12 waiting for and hastening the coming of the day of God, because of which the heavens will be set on fire

and dissolved, and the heavenly bodies will melt as they burn!

1 John 2:8 (ESV) the darkness is passing away and the true light is already shining.

1 John 2:17 (BLB) And the world is passing away, and its desire; but the one doing the will of God abides to the age.

1 John 2:18 (ESV) and as you have heard that antichrist is coming, so now many antichrists have come. Therefore we know that it is the last hour. (Compare Matthew 24:23-34)

1 John 4:3 (BLB) and every spirit that does not confess Jesus is not of God, and this is that of the antichrist, which you heard that is coming, and now is already in the world. (Compare 2 Thessalonians 2:7)

Jude 1:4,14-15 (ESV) For certain people have crept in unnoticed who long ago were designated for this condemnation... It was also about these that Enoch, the seventh from Adam, prophesied, saying, "Behold, the Lord comes with ten thousands of his holy ones, 15 to execute judgment on all and to convict all the ungodly of all their deeds

Jude 1:17-19 (ESV) But you must remember, beloved, the predictions of the apostles of our Lord Jesus Christ. 18 They said to you, "In the last time there will be scoffers, following their own ungodly passions." 19 It is these who cause divisions...

Revelation 1:1 (ESV) ...which God gave him to show to his servants the things that must soon take place

Revelation 1:3 (ESV) for the time is near.

Revelation 2:25 (ESV) Only hold fast what you have until I come.

Revelation 3:10 (LSV) I also will keep you from the hour of the trial that is about to come on all the world, to try those dwelling on the earth.

Revelation 3:11 (ESV) I am coming soon. Hold fast what you have, so that no one may seize your crown.

Revelation 12:5 (LSV) and she brought forth a male son, who is about to rule all the nations with a rod of iron

Revelation 18:24 (ESV) And in her [the Great City Babylon] was found the blood of prophets and of saints, and of all who have been slain on earth. (Compare Matthew 23:35-36; Luke 11:50-51)

Revelation 22:6 (ESV) "These words are trustworthy and true. And the Lord, the God of the spirits of the prophets, has sent his angel to show his servants what must soon take place."

Revelation 22:7 (ESV) And behold, I am coming soon.

Revelation 22:10 (ESV) Do not seal up the words of the prophecy of this book, for the time is near. (Compare Dan. 8:26)

Revelation 22:12 (ESV) Behold, I am coming soon.

Revelation 22:20 (ESV) "Surely I am coming soon."

Chapter 4
An Alternate Perspective

Some of the earliest church fathers believed that at least a part of the Olivet Discourse and Revelation happened in the first century. Early church father Andreas of Caesarea, writing sometime between 563 – 637 AD, stated:

> Our Lord foretold the future events to the apostles who were asking about the destruction of the Temple in Jerusalem and about the end of time, as much as they were able to receive. These things already happened, in the siege of Vespasian and Titus, to the Judeans who killed Christ, just as Josephus the Hebrew narrates.[29]

Early church father Eusebius Pamphili of Caesarea, in his series *Church History*, written around 325 AD, said that the prophecy of the Great Tribulation spoken by Jesus was fulfilled in the events of the war recorded by Josephus.

> 6.And then, as if speaking concerning the people, he says, For there shall be great distress in the land, and wrath upon this people. And they shall fall by the edge of the sword, and shall be led away captive into all nations. And Jerusalem shall be trodden down of the Gentiles, until the times of the Gentiles be fulfilled. And again: When you shall see Jerusalem compassed with armies, then know that the desolation thereof is nigh.

---

[29]Caesarea, Andrew of. Commentary on the Apocalypse. Translated by Eugenia Scarvellis Constantinou, Catholic University of America Press, 2017, https://preteristarchives.org/andreas-of-caesarea/, 100.

> 7.If any one compares the words of our Saviour with the other accounts of the historian [Josephus] concerning the whole war, how can one fail to wonder, and to admit that the foreknowledge and the prophecy of our Saviour were truly divine and marvellously strange.[30]

In the 1800s, several scholars in America said that most or all of Revelation happened in the first century. They believed the world was entering a new era of peace and prosperity.

The belief that the Great Tribulation is expected in our near future first became popular in the early 1900s, just before World War I. A few years before World War I, Cyrus I. Scofield published the Scofield Reference Bible. His book promoted a unique view of the end times which taught that Scofield's generation was the last to live. It taught terrible things would happen to the world in fulfillment of Bible prophecy and Christ's return. At first, readers mocked his view as unscholarly. Still, as the Great Depression, World War I, and World War II hit, his theory seemed completely vindicated and became the dominant view in the American church. Even Israel became a state in 1948. Christian writers Hal Lindsey (*The Late Great Planet Earth*), Edgar C. Whisenant (*88 Reasons Why The Rapture Will Be in 1988*), and Tim LaHaye (*Left Behind*) inspired most American churches that their generation was the last one.

---

[30] Eusebius, Church History, 3.7.6-7, https://www.historytimeline.org/docs/eusebius/church_history/book_03.php.

Past Fulfillment

There is an alternate belief system that traces its roots back to the 1800s. It interprets the time statements of the Bible literally, and it argues that Jesus promised to return in his generation and actually did. This view teaches that the scripture means what it says: the Great Tribulation, the end times, and the general resurrection of the dead were promised to come in the first century and occurred on time. It does not expect a return of Christ in our future.

Today, Christians who adhere to the belief of a past fulfillment don't all agree on which events of Revelation were fulfilled. Most agree that all except the final three chapters of Revelation happened in the first century.

Some, including myself, hold that every prophecy in Revelation was promised to occur soon (to the first century audience) or have eternal ongoing fulfillment and that all were fulfilled or established shortly after the book of Revelation was written, as promised. Those holding the fulfilled view believe modern day teachings from the Scofield Bible, for example, have misguided many Christians with assumptions based on a worldview of what the "new heavens and earth," "resurrection of the dead," "defeat of death," and "end of the age" mean. Christians believing the fulfilled prophecy view dismiss twenty-first century teachings of Scofield, choosing instead to let the Bible interpret itself.

Many believers who are acquainted with the view of a past fulfillment but have not looked deeply into the matter find this interpretation of scripture to be offensive or even blasphemous (including myself, for a period of eight years).

If one can question preconceived notions taught to them, read the scriptures for what they actually say, and research the history of first century Israel, they will discover that the fulfilled view is not only plausible, but the most likely to be true. Except for their views of the end, these Christians generally hold the same beliefs as most Christians in their varied denominations.

"Can one still be a Christian and believe Christ already returned?" Yes! The vast majority of those holding the view of a past return trust in Jesus as Lord and Savior, believe he died for sinners on the cross, rose again, and is God incarnate. They hold that the Bible is the infallible word of God and that it should be trusted above man's opinion or doctrine. They believe the gospel message is very much for today, and that fear of future "end-times" can paralyze the church, making some Christians unproductive members of society.

While the notion of a past return of Christ is still unpopular, it can be shown that this perspective more naturally and sensibly interprets the texts of the Bible and explains many mysteries that continue to baffle scholars.

If Jesus did promise to return in his generation, does the first century contain any history that proves Jesus and his angels came on the clouds? This will be explored in the next section.

Chapter 5
Who Saw His Return?

Most Christians are unaware of a remarkable event that took place in 66 AD. At that time, some reliable historians documented angelic armies coming on the clouds in fiery chariots against Jerusalem. The variations in the documentation show that this data did not all come from the same source. Josephus, a Jewish historian writing in 75 AD, said:

> "Besides these [signs], a few days after that feast, on the one- and-twentieth day of the month Artemisius, [Jyar,] a certain prodigious and incredible phenomenon appeared; I suppose the account of it would seem to be a fable, were it not related by those that saw it, and were not the events that followed it of so considerable a nature as to deserve such signals; for, before sun-setting, chariots and troops of soldiers in their armour were seen running about among the clouds, and surrounding of cities. Moreover, at that feast which we call Pentecost, as the priests were going by night into the inner [court of the] temple, as their custom was, to perform their sacred ministrations, they said that, in the first place, they felt a quaking, and heard a great noise, and after that they heard a sound as of a great multitude, saying, "Let us remove hence"[31]

---

[31] Josephus, Flavius, Samuel Burder, and William Whiston. 2015. The Genuine Works of Flavius Josephus, the Jewish Historian: Containing Twenty Books of the Jewish Antiquities, Seven Books of the Jewish War, and the Life of Josephus. N.p.: Creative Media Partners, LLC. http://penelope.uchicago.edu/josephus/index.html, 6.5.3, http://penelope.uchicago.edu/josephus/war-6.html.

Josephus is the most well-known Jewish historian of his time. He was a Jewish priest and general during the war in 67 AD. After receiving a prophetic dream of the Jews' destruction, he promised to serve as a minister of God and surrendered to the Romans.[32] Immediately after, God miraculously delivered him from a life-threatening situation.[33] Josephus later became a historian dedicated to unbiasedly recording the events he witnessed during the war.[34] Churches, historians, preachers, and seminary schools quote and validate his works.

Tacitus, a Roman historian, and senator, writing between 100-110 AD, also stated that angelic armies were seen on the clouds:

> Prodigies had occurred, which this nation, prone to superstition, but hating all religious rites, did not deem it lawful to expiate by offering and sacrifice. There had been seen hosts joining battle in the skies, the fiery gleam of arms, the temple illuminated by a sudden radiance from the clouds. The doors of the inner shrine were suddenly thrown open, and a voice of more than mortal tone was heard to cry that the Gods were departing. At the same instant there was a mighty stir as of departure. Some few put a fearful meaning on these events, but in most there was a firm persuasion, that in the ancient records of their priests was contained a prediction of how at this very time

---

[32] Josephus, War, 3.8.3, http://penelope.uchicago.edu/josephus/war-3.html.

[33] Josephus, War, 3.8.4-8.

[34] Josephus, War, Preface, http://penelope.uchicago.edu/josephus/war-pref.html.

> the East was to grow powerful, and rulers, coming from Judæa, were to acquire universal empire.[35]

Tacitus was a Roman senator and historian and is considered one of the greatest Roman historians of his time. He despised Christianity and was known to be careful, skeptical, and factual in his works. One of his duties was to supervise foreign religious cults in Rome. Historians use his works to validate the crucifixion of Christ.

Sepher Yosippon, a work by an anonymous Jew writing in the tenth century, wrote that these angelic armies in 66 AD were horses and riders of fire.

> Moreover, in those days were seen chariots of fire and horsemen, a great force flying across the sky low to the ground coming against Jerusalem and all the land of Judah, all of them horses of fire and riders of fire.[36]

The anonymous Pseudo-Hegesippus, estimated to have been written between 370-375 AD, also described this event and mentioned a tremendous figure leading the army.

> Also after many days a certain figure appeared of tremendous size, which many saw, just as the books of the

---

[35] Tacitus, Cornelius. 2011. The, complete works of Tacitus, The annals. The History. The life of Cnaeus Julius Agricola. Germany and its, tribes. A dialogue on oratory. Edited by Sara Bryant and Moses Hadas. Translated by Alfred J. Church and William J. Brodribb. Medford, Massachusetts: Perseus Project. http://data.perseus.org/catalog/urn:cts:latinLit:phi1351.phi004.perseus-eng1, 5.13, https://www.perseus.tufts.edu/hopper/text?doc=Perseus%3Atext%3A1999.02.0080%3Abook%3D5%3Achapter%3D13.

[36]Yosippon, Mediaeval History, 87, http://fulfilledtheology.ning.com/forum/topics/historical-records-with-some.

> Jews have disclosed, and before the setting of the sun there were suddenly seen in the clouds chariots [p. 393] and armed battle arrays, by which the cities of all Iudaea [Judea] and its territories were invaded.[37]

It is not difficult to imagine that Christ was leading this army of angels against Jerusalem.

Will Every Eye See Him?

Some Bible translations indicate that all the world would see Christ's return.

> Matthew 24:30 (NIV) Then will appear the sign of the Son of Man in heaven. And then **all the peoples [phulé] of the earth** will mourn when they see the Son of Man coming on the clouds of heaven, with power and great glory.

However, this may be a mistranslation. This Greek word for "peoples" is "phulé,"[38] which is commonly translated as "tribes" throughout the Bible.

> Matthew 19:28 (NIV) you who have followed me will also sit on twelve thrones, judging the twelve **tribes [phulé]** of Israel

---

[37] Pseudo. 2005. Hegesippus, translated from Latin into English. Translated by Wade Blocker. (This excerpt is taken from the Latin edited by Vincent Ussani) ed. https://www.tertullian.org/fathers/hegesippus_00_eintro.htm, 5.44, https://www.tertullian.org/fathers/hegesippus_05_book5.htm.

[38] "Matthew 24:30 Greek Text Analysis." n.d. Bible Hub. Accessed December 9, 2022. https://biblehub.com/text/matthew/24-30.htm.

The word "earth," or "gé,"[39] means "the earth, soil, land, region, country, inhabitants of a region" and sometimes describes the land of Israel (Matthew 2:6,20-21). The International Standard Version translates this passage as follows:

> Matthew 24:30 (ISV) Then the sign of the Son of Man will appear in the sky, and all '**the tribes of the land** will mourn' when they see 'the Son of Man coming on the clouds of heaven' with power and great glory.

In the above translation, "tribes of the land" can be identified as the twelve Jewish tribes of Israel rather than "nations of the earth." The same is true for Luke 21:35, where Young's Literal Translation translates "the whole earth" as "land."

> Luke 21:35 (YLT) for as a snare it shall come on all those dwelling **on the face of all the land**

Jesus compared the visibility of his return to a lightning strike.

> Matthew 24:27 (ESV) For as the lightning comes from the east and shines as far as the west, so will be the coming of the Son of Man.

Lightning is not visible across the entire planet but is limited to a geographical region such as the land of Israel.

Moreover, Jesus said they could escape this tribulation by fleeing Judea to the mountains.

> Matthew 24:15-18 (ESV) "So when you see the abomination of desolation spoken of by the prophet Daniel, standing in the holy place (let the reader understand), 16 then let **those**

---

[39] "Strong's Greek: 1093. γῆ (gé) -- the earth, land." n.d. Bible Hub. Accessed December 9, 2022. https://biblehub.com/greek/1093.htm.

> **who are in Judea flee to the mountains.** 17 Let the one who is on the housetop not go down to take what is in his house, 18 and let the one who is in the field not turn back to take his cloak.

Jesus could not have a distant end-of-the-world destruction in mind when only those in Judea needed to flee to find safety in the mountains, proving that it was a localized event.

Only those in Judea would witness his return and the twelve tribes of Israel would mourn, not the entire world.

While a first-century return of Christ may seem plausible, Jesus promised to resurrect and judge the living and the dead when he returned (Matthew 16:27-28; John 14:2-3; 1 Corinthians 15:23; Colossians 3:4; 1 Thessalonians 4:16; 2 Timothy 4:1). Since these end-time events are promised simultaneously, one must consider how the resurrection could have happened in the first century.

Chapter 6
The First Century Resurrection

For centuries, Christians have debated where believers go when they die and what happens in the resurrection of the dead. Most believe that upon death, believers go to heaven without receiving their resurrected bodies. They await a future resurrection when they will return to their renewed physical bodies and live eternally either on earth, in heaven, or in a merged state of both. However, this view makes it easy to reject the idea of a first-century return of Christ, as promised in the Bible.

Jesus and the apostles testified to their first-century audiences that Jesus was about to return and resurrect the dead:

> 2 Timothy 4:1 (LSV) I fully testify, then, before God, and the Lord **Jesus Christ, who is about to judge [the] living and dead at His appearing** and His Kingdom

> Matthew 16:27-28 (GNT) For **the Son of Man is about to come** in the glory of his Father with his angels, **and then he will reward each one according to his deeds.** I assure you that there are some here who will not die until they have seen the Son of Man come as King.

> Acts 24:15 (LSV) having hope toward God, which they themselves also wait for, [that] **there is about to be a resurrection of the dead, both of righteous and unrighteous**;

> 1 Peter 4:4-7 (ESV) With respect to this they are surprised when you do not join them in the same flood of

debauchery, and they malign you; 5 **but they will give account** to him **who is ready to judge the living and the dead**. 6 For this is why the gospel was preached even to those who are dead, that though judged in the flesh the way people are, they might live in the spirit the way God does. 7 **The end of all things is at hand**; therefore be self-controlled and sober-minded for the sake of your prayers.

See also 1 Corinthians 15:23; Colossians 3:4; 1 Thessalonians 4:16; John 14:2-3.

With the above promises of Christ's imminent return and resurrection of the dead, it is important to carefully examine what the Bible teaches will happen in the resurrection and consider historical records that may fulfill the Bible's expectations within the lifetime of the apostles.

According to the Bible, the resurrection of the saints involves three things:

1. waiting in Sheol/Hades until the general resurrection of the dead (Genesis 37:35; Psalm 9:17; 31:17; 49:14; 88:3; Isaiah 5:14; 38:10; Psalms 16:10; John 3:13; Acts 2:29,31,34; 1 Samuel 2:6; Job 14:10-14; Isaiah 26:19; Daniel 12:2,13; John 5:28-29; 6:39-40; 11:24-25; 1 Corinthians 15:16,18,20,51-52; 1 Corinthians 15:54-55 [WEB]; 1 Thessalonians 4:13-15; 5:10; Hebrews 11:39-40; 1 Peter 1:5,8-9; Revelation 20:13)

2. rising in heavenly, spiritual bodies that can be visible, invisible, or semi-visible (Luke 20:35-36; 1 Corinthians 15:35,44,49; Philippians 3:20-21)

3. ascending into heaven where saints remain forever (John 14:2-3; 15:19; 17:14,16,24; 2 Corinthians 4:14; 5:1-2; Philippians 3:20; 1 Thessalonians 4:17; Hebrews 11:16,40; 1 Peter 1:4)

A supernatural event occurring in 66 AD meets the above expectations and was documented by Cassius Dio, Josephus, and the anonymous Sepher Yosippon.

For two thousand years, Christians have been going to heaven, as evidenced by Near Death Experiences.[40] This only happens because the resurrection of the dead took place on time and saints have received their heavenly, resurrected bodies.

The following sections will approach the scriptures with a fresh perspective and a willingness to challenge traditional assumptions. This approach is necessary to gain a comprehensive understanding of the nature of the resurrection and its fulfillment in the first century.

Destined for Sheol

The Old Testament says the righteous and wicked alike would be sent to a place called Sheol (Genesis 37:35; Psalm 9:17;

---

[40] Habermas, Gary R. 2016. "Near Death Experiences: Evidence for an Afterlife? - Apologetics." North American Mission Board. https://www.namb.net/apologetics/resource/near-death-experiences-evidence-for-an-afterlife/; Long, Jeffrey. 2014. "Near-Death Experiences Evidence for Their Reality." NCBI. https://www.ncbi.nlm.nih.gov/pmc/articles/PMC6172100/; Williams, Kevin. 2019. "Scientific Evidence Supporting Near-Death Experiences and the Afterlife." Near-Death; Experiences and the Afterlife. https://near-death.com/afterlife-evidence/; Zaimov, Stoyan. 2016. "Do Thousands of Near-Death Experiences Prove Heaven Is Real?" Christian Post. https://www.christianpost.com/news/near-death-experiences-prove-heaven-is-real-pastor-john-burke.html.

31:17; 49:14; 88:3; Isaiah 5:14; 38:10) or its Greek equivalent "Hades" (Psalms 16:10; Acts 2:31). They did not ascend to heaven (John 3:13; Acts 2:29,34; Hebrews 11:39-40).

> Psalm 9:17 (ESV) The wicked shall return to Sheol, all the nations that forget God.

> Isaiah 38:10 (ESV) I said, In the middle of my days I must depart; I am consigned to the gates of Sheol for the rest of my years.

> John 3:13 (ESV) No one has ascended into heaven except he who descended from heaven, the Son of Man.

> Acts 2:34 (ESV) For David did not ascend into the heavens

The Bible describes the afterlife in Sheol/Hades as a sleep (Job 3:11,13; 14:12; Psalm 13:3; John 11:11-13; Acts 13:36; 1 Corinthians 11:30 [NIV]).

> Psalm 13:3 (ESV) Consider and answer me, O Lord my God; light up my eyes, lest I sleep the sleep of death

> John 11:11-13 (ESV) After saying these things, he said to them, "Our friend Lazarus has fallen asleep, but I go to awaken him." The disciples said to him, "Lord, if he has fallen asleep, he will recover." Now Jesus had spoken of his death, but they thought that he meant taking rest in sleep.

> 1 Corinthians 11:30 (NIV) That is why many among you are weak and sick, and a number of you have fallen asleep.

As when sleeping, those who slept in Sheol/Hades were unconscious and unaware of the passage of time (Psalm 6:5; 17:15; 30:9; 31:17; 88:11; 115:17; 146:4; Ecclesiastes 9:5-6,10; Isaiah 38:18-19).

> Psalm 6:5 (ESV) For in death there is no remembrance of you; in Sheol who will give you praise?

> Ecclesiastes 9:5-6,10 (ESV) For the living know that they will die, but the dead know nothing, and they have no more reward, for the memory of them is forgotten. Their love and their hate and their envy have already perished, and forever they have no more share in all that is done under the sun... 10 Whatever your hand finds to do, do it with your might, for there is no work or thought or knowledge or wisdom in Sheol, to which you are going.

> Isaiah 38:18-19 (ESV) For Sheol does not thank you; death does not praise you; those who go down to the pit do not hope for your faithfulness. The living, the living, he thanks you, as I do this day; the father makes known to the children your faithfulness.

God did not intend for mankind to descend into Sheol/Hades. Adam brought this afterlife death upon us when he ate the forbidden fruit (Genesis 2:17).

The Resurrection Awakening

Just like those who sleep will wake up in the morning, God promised to wake up mankind from Hades at the resurrection on the "last day" (1 Samuel 2:6; Job 14:10-14; Isaiah 26:19; Daniel 12:2,13; John 5:28-29; 6:39-40; 11:24-25; 1 Corinthians 15:16,18,20,51-52; 1 Corinthians 15:54-55 [WEB]; 1 Thessalonians 4:13-15; 5:10; 1 Peter 1:5,8-9; Revelation 20:13).

Job did not expect to leave Sheol until the resurrection.

> Job 14:10-14 (ESV) But a man dies and is laid low; man breathes his last, and where is he? 11 As waters fail from a

lake and a river wastes away and dries up, 12 so a man lies down and rises not again; **till the heavens are no more he will not awake** or be roused out of his sleep. 13 Oh that you would hide me in **Sheol**, that you would conceal me **until your wrath be past**, that you would **appoint me a set time, and remember me**! 14 **If a man dies, shall he live again?** All the days of my service I would wait, **till my renewal should come.**

Daniel would not stand again until the "end of days."

> Daniel 12:13 (ESV) But go your way **till the end**. And you **shall rest and shall stand** in your allotted place **at the end of the days.**

Jesus said he would raise the dead on the last day.

> John 6:39-40 (ESV) And this is the will of him who sent me, that I should lose nothing of all that he has given me, but **raise it up on the last day**. For this is the will of my Father, that everyone who looks on the Son and believes in him should have eternal life, and **I will raise him up on the last day**."

> John 11:24-25 (ESV) Martha said to him, "**I know that he will rise again in the resurrection on the last day**." Jesus said to her, "I am the resurrection and the life. Whoever believes in me, though he die, yet shall he live..."

Peter was expecting the salvation of Christian souls from Hades in the last time.

> 1 Peter 1:5,8-9 (WEB) who by the power of God are guarded through faith **for a salvation ready to be revealed in the last time**... 8 whom, not having known, you love. In him, though now you don't see him, yet believing, you rejoice

greatly with joy that is unspeakable and full of glory, 9 **receiving the result of your faith, the salvation of your souls.**

The saints were not expected to wake from Hades until the general resurrection of the dead at the "last day."

When did Hades End?

Most Christians believe correctly that after they die, they will go to heaven. However, they may not realize that this is only possible because Hades was defeated when Christ returned and resurrected the dead in 66 AD. They assume all saints began going to heaven after the cross.

It is important to understand that the resurrection of the "last day" did not happen at the time of the cross. Even after the cross, most saints remained in Hades for a while and expected a future resurrection, as confirmed by the apostle Paul ("most" will be explained in the next chapter). He wrote that Christians still slept at death (1 Corinthians 11:30; 15:6,18,20,51; 1 Thessalonians 4:13-15). Additionally, Christians were promised to rise from "Hades," not heaven in the approaching resurrection of the dead.

> 1 Corinthians 15:54-55 (WEB) But when this perishable body will have become imperishable, and this mortal will have put on immortality, then what is written will happen: "Death is swallowed up in victory."Isaiah 25:8
>
> "Death, where is your sting? **Hades**, where is your victory?"See Hosea 13:14

> Revelation 20:13 (ESV) And the sea gave up the dead who were in it, Death and **Hades** gave up the dead who were in them, and they were judged, each one of them, according to what they had done.

Moreover, Paul said that without a resurrection of the dead, those who slept in Christ had perished. Someone who has perished could not be conscious in God's presence.

> 1 Corinthians 15:16,18,20 (ESV) For if the dead are not raised... 18 **Then those also who have fallen asleep in Christ have perished**... 20 But in fact Christ has been raised from the dead, the firstfruits of those who have fallen asleep.

Resurrection, by definition, means something dead coming back to life. No one living in heaven is considered "dead" according to Biblical standards, otherwise one would have to assume Jesus died when he ascended into heaven. Hence, the Bible never says Christians are "resurrected" from heaven.

Even after the cross, the dead saints remained in Hades and did not go to heaven until Christ's return and the resurrection in 66 AD.

The Inaccessibility of Heaven

The Bible teaches that heaven was not accessible to the saints until they had been resurrected. Jesus explicitly told the disciples that they could not enter heaven until he returned for them in the resurrection.

> John 13:36 (WEB) Jesus answered, "**Where I am going, you can't follow now, but you will follow afterwards.**"

Jesus was going to his father's house or heaven (John 14:2,12,28; 16:28).

> John 14:2-3 (WEB) In my Father's house are many homes. If it weren't so, I would have told you. I am going to prepare a place for you. 3 If I go and prepare a place for you, I will come again, and will receive you to myself; that where I am, you may be there also.

The departure of Jesus to his father's house refers to his ascension to heaven, which occurred forty days after the cross (John 16:7; Acts 1:9-11; 2:1-4). The disciples would follow Christ into heaven when Jesus returned to resurrect the dead, give eternal life, and to bring his followers into the houses he had built for them (John 14:3,18-19; 16:16; 17:24). Only after the resurrection would believers be brought into Christ's presence and forever be with the Lord.

> 2 Corinthians 4:14 (ESV) knowing that he who raised the Lord Jesus will raise us also with Jesus **and bring us with you into his presence**.

> 1 Thessalonians 4:16-17 (ESV) For the Lord himself will descend from heaven with a cry of command, with the voice of an archangel, and with the sound of the trumpet of God. And the dead in Christ will rise first. Then we who are alive, who are left, will be caught up together with them in the clouds to meet the Lord in the air, **and so we will always be with the Lord**.

Additionally, Hebrews prophesied that the heavenly city Christ was building for the saints was "about" to be available.

Hebrews 11:16,40 (ESV) But as it is, they desire a better country, that is, a heavenly one. Therefore God is not ashamed to be called their God, for he has prepared for them a city... since God had provided something better for us, that apart from us they should not be made perfect.

Hebrews 13:14 (DBH) For here we have no abiding city, but instead seek the one **about to come**.

Hebrews said the way into heaven remained undisclosed until the coming age arrived. The Jewish temple, which stood in the first century, symbolized the "present age" (Old Covenant age), and when the temple would fall, the "Holy Place" or "heaven" would become available.

Hebrews 9:8-9 (WEB) The Holy Spirit is indicating this, that the way into the Holy Place wasn't yet revealed while the first tabernacle was still standing. 9 This is a symbol of the present age

(The present age was the Old Covenant age, while the age to come was the exclusive New Covenant age [Hebrews 8:13].)

Hebrews used the term "holy place" to describe heaven itself.

Hebrews 8:1-2 (ESV) we have such a high priest, one who is seated at the right hand of the throne of the Majesty **in heaven, a minister in the holy places**, in the true tent that the Lord set up, not man.

Hebrews 9:24 (WEB) **For Christ hasn't entered into holy places made with hands**, which are representations of the true, **but into heaven itself**, now to appear in the presence of God for us;

The scriptures agree that heaven was not open to the dead saints until Jesus returned to resurrect them and end the Old Covenant age at the destruction of the temple.

In Paradise That Day?

Some scholars believe in a future resurrection but argue that believers go to heaven today without needing to wait for a resurrection. To support this view, they may cite the passage where Jesus promised the thief on the cross that the thief would be with Jesus in paradise before the resurrection.

> Luke 23:43 (NIV) Jesus answered him, "Truly I tell you, **today** you will be with me in paradise."

Everywhere else it is used, "paradise" represents heaven, that is, the Garden of Eden (Revelation 2:7) and the third heaven (2 Corinthians 12:2-3). However, this argument is weakened by its dependence on the placement of an uninspired comma. When translated with the comma in its traditional position, it leads to a contradictory statement. The Bible says that Jesus descended into Hades when he died, not heaven (Psalm 16:10; Matthew 12:40; Acts 2:31; Ephesians 4:8-9). Jesus explicitly said he was not in heaven when he died.

> John 20:17 (ESV) Jesus said to her, "Do not cling to me, for I have not yet ascended to the Father; but go to my brothers and say to them, 'I am ascending to my Father and your Father, to my God and your God.'"

The thief could not be with Jesus in paradise that same day if Jesus was not there on that day. This contradiction can be solved when one realizes that the original Greek text did not have commas, though it sometimes had pauses represented by dots. Translators added commas to the translation several hundred years later; hence, they are uninspired. If one moves the comma forward, as might be permissible, he gets:

> Luke 23:43 (WEB) Jesus said to him, "Assuredly I tell you today, you will be with me in Paradise."

(In the above WEB passage, the comma has been moved from before "today" to after "today.")

To further support this, the earliest Greek manuscripts contain a pause, the equivalent of a comma, after "today," making the phrase, "Truly I tell you today [pause or comma]..."

In his article, "The Significance of a Comma: An Analysis of Luke 23:43,"[41] Wilson Paroschi, Ph.D. makes this point and illustrates how placing the comma after today is highly consistent with Luke's literary style.

Greek scholar E.W. Bullinger in his book *The Rich Man and Lazarus: An Intermediate State?* says, "I say unto thee this day," was a well-known Hebrew idiom to emphasize the seriousness and importance of the words (Deuteronomy 4:26,29,40; 5:6; 6:6; 7:11; 8:1,11,19; 9:3; 10:13; 11:2,8,13,18,27,28,32; 13:18; 15:5; 19:9; 26:3,17,18; 27:1,4,10; 28:1,13,14,15; 24:12;

---

[41] Paroschi, Wilson, and Engenheiro Coelho. 2013. "The Significance of a Comma: An Analysis of Luke 23:43." Ministry Magazine. https://www.ministrymagazine.org/archive/2013/06/the-significance-of-a-comma:-an-analysis-of-luke-23:43.

30:2,8,11,15,16,18; 32:46; Acts 20:26).[42] Luke used the phrase in the same way in Acts.

> Acts 20:26-27 (ESV) **Therefore I testify to you this day** that I am innocent of the blood of all, for I did not shrink from declaring to you the whole counsel of God.

> Acts 24:21 (ESV) other than this one thing that I cried out while standing among them: 'It is with respect to the resurrection of the dead that I am on trial before you **this day**.'"

Bullinger points out that in similar situations (Luke 4:21; 19:9) when Luke wants "today" to belong to the following phrase instead of with the verb "say," he separates the two words with "that" or, in Greek, "hoti."

> Luke 4:21 (ESV) And he began to **say** to them, [**that**] "**Today** this Scripture has been fulfilled in your hearing."

> Luke 19:9 (ESV) And Jesus **said** to him, [**that**] "**Today** salvation has come to this house, since he also is a son of Abraham.

In Luke 23:43, he does **not** say, "Truly I tell you **that** today you will be with me in paradise," which he would have done if he wanted to join "today" with the following phrase.

The thief asked Jesus to remember him when his kingdom came (Luke 23:42), and Jesus wanted to emphasize that it would certainly happen. All indicators point to the fact that the

---

[42] Bullinger, Ethelbert W. 1902. The Rich Man and Lazarus: An Intermediate State? https://www.afterlife.co.nz/wp-content/uploads/2009/07/eb-rml1.pdf, 22.

thief was promised to ascend to paradise when Jesus returned with his kingdom, not immediately upon his death.

Until their resurrection came to pass, the dead saints could not ascend into heaven.

Irenaeus on Hades

Some Christians consider the writings of the early church fathers to be almost as inspired as the Bible itself. They say Christians should reject a past second coming of Christ and past general resurrection because it does not adhere to the early church fathers' teachings. However, according to one prominent early church father, if the resurrection has not happened, Christians go to Hades and not heaven when they die today.

The early church father Irenaeus, writing sometime between 175 and 185 AD, said it was heretical to believe that Christians would enter heaven upon their deaths before the resurrection and must instead wait in Hades for their immortal bodies.[43]

Perhaps those hoping not to contradict the early church fathers have not realized this means Christians should not expect to go to heaven when they die.

---

[43]Irenaeus. 1885. Against Heresies, Ante-Nicene Fathers. Edited by James Donaldson, A. C. Coxe., and Kevin Knight. Translated by Alexander Roberts and William Rambaut. Vol. 1. Buffalo, NY: Christian Literature Publishing Co. https://www.newadvent.org/fathers/0103.htm, 5.31.1-2, http://www.newadvent.org/fathers/0103531.htm.

Irenaeus predicted the resurrection would occur at the fall of the Roman empire,[44] but only the inspired Bible is entirely trustworthy. If the Bible teaches the necessity of a first-century resurrection, believers should place their confidence in what the scriptures say above man's uninspired opinions.

The Resurrection Body

The Bible promised the saints heavenly, glorified, spiritual bodies like Christ and the angels in the general resurrection.

> 1 Corinthians 15:35,44,49 (ESV) How are the dead raised? **With what kind of body will they come?** ...44 It is sown a natural body; **it is raised a spiritual body** ...49 Just as we have borne the image of the man of dust, **we shall also bear the image of the man of heaven**

> Luke 20:35-36 (NIV) But those who are considered worthy of taking part in the age to come and in the resurrection from the dead will neither marry nor be given in marriage, 36 and they can no longer die; **for they are like the angels**.

> Philippians 3:20-21 (ESV) But our citizenship is in heaven, and from it we await a Savior, the Lord Jesus Christ, 21 **who will transform our lowly body to be like his glorious body**, by the power that enables him even to subject all things to himself.

Paul and Christ said believers would have heavenly/spiritual bodies like Jesus' glorious body and the angels. Therefore, one

---

[44] Irenaeus, Against Heresies, 5.26, http://www.newadvent.org/fathers/0103526.htm.

can examine the qualities of the bodies of Christ and the angels to understand what kind of bodies the saints will have.

Christ and angels have bodies that are usually invisible and intangible but can become visible, tangible, or in-between on certain occasions.

Christ's body "disappeared from their sight" (Luke 24:31) and was "suddenly standing among them" (John 20:26) but could also be seen and touched by Thomas (Luke 24:37-39; John 20:26-29), and he ascended to heaven where he is to this day in this same body (Acts 1:9-11).

Angels likewise had spiritual/heavenly bodies that were at times tangible as shown in these passages:

- the Lord ate bread with Abraham by the oaks of Mamre (Genesis 18:1-21)
- the two angels in Sodom and Gomorrah appeared as men (Genesis 19:1-11)
- Jacob wrestled with God (Genesis 32:22-32)
- Elisha's vision of angels (2 Kings 6:17)
- the donkey could see the angel but Balaam could not until the angel turned visible (Numbers 22:22-33)
- God's voice sounding like thunder when Jesus was baptized (Matthew 3:16-17) or again before Jesus died (John 12:28-29)
- Mary talked with two angels standing at Jesus' tomb (John 20:12)

The Bible said that saints would have bodies like Christ and the angels; hence, the saints will have immortal, resurrected bodies that can be invisible, visible, intangible, or tangible as the Lord wills.

Where is Home?

Scholars debate over where Christians end up after the general resurrection. Some say earth, others heaven, still others say earth and heaven merged. The Bible indicates Christians do not live on earth forever when it says they are not of this world (John 15:19; John 17:14,16). Jesus explicitly said he was preparing a place for them in heaven.

> John 14:2-3 (ESV) In my Father's house are many rooms. If it were not so, would I have told you that I go to prepare a place for you? And if I go and prepare a place for you, I will come again and will take you to myself, that where I am you may be also.

When Jesus said "I will come again... and will take you to myself," he meant that when he returned, he would resurrect and bring the disciples into heaven or his "Father's house," where he had prepared them rooms. *(It should be noted that the above passage also implies that the disciples and the contemporary believers would not enter heaven until Christ returned and resurrected them.)* The New Testament gives other indications that heaven is the Christian's final destination. In the resurrection:

- Christians will be with Christ where he is (John 17:24)

- God will bring saints into Jesus' presence (2 Corinthians 4:14)
- Believers will live in a house "eternal in the heavens" (2 Corinthians 5:1-2)
- Their citizenship will be in heaven (Philippians 3:20)
- Christians will always be with the Lord in the clouds (1 Thessalonians 4:17)
- They will receive a heavenly city (Hebrews 11:16,40)
- Their inheritance will be in heaven (1 Peter 1:4).

One is logically led to conclude that believers will not dwell upon the earth, or earth and heaven merged, but in heaven.

Jesus, The Resurrection Model

Jesus is the resurrection model. His resurrection demonstrates the kind of resurrection the saints will have.

> Romans 6:5 (ESV) For if we have been united with him in a death like his, we shall certainly be united with him in a resurrection like his.

Jesus descended into Hades, was resurrected in a spiritual, heavenly body, and ascended into heaven.

1. He descended into Hades when he died (Psalm 16:10; Matthew 12:40; John 20:17; Acts 2:31; Ephesians 4:8-9).
2. He rose again in a spiritual, glorious, heavenly body (Luke 24:13-35; John 20:15,26; 21:4; Philippians 3:21).

3. He ascended into heaven (Acts 1:9-11; Ephesians 4:8-9) where he remains to this day.

Likewise, the saints would sleep in Hades until the day they were resurrected in their spiritual, heavenly bodies and ascend into heaven.

Resurrection in History

Jesus promised the resurrection in his disciples' lifetime, so is there any historical record showing it occurred on time? Suppose the saints come from an invisible place (Hades), end up in another hidden place (heaven), and are resurrected in spiritual bodies that may or may not be visible. In that case, it is much easier to find a fulfillment in history. Fortunately, a semi-visible event occurred in 66 AD, the same year that angelic armies arrived on the clouds. Morais states:

> When the Jewish revolt began, Nero was in Greece building a canal. Concerning the construction of this waterway, Cassius Dio writes, "[W]hen the first workers touched the earth, blood spouted from it, groans and bellowings were heard, and many phantoms appeared. Nero himself thereupon grasped a mattock and by throwing up some of the soil fairly compelled the rest to imitate him." [Cassius Dio Roman History 63.16] In recording this event, Suetonius indicates that as Nero broke the ground the sound of a trumpet was heard. [Suetonius Lives of the Twelve Caesars 6.19.] The fact that a trumpet was heard at the time in which the dead appear to have been raised clearly fulfills 1 Corinthians 15:52: "For the trumpet will

sound, [and] the dead will be raised imperishable..."[45] (footnotes were translated to references)

Josephus wrote,

> Besides these [signs], a few days after that feast, on the one-and-twentieth day of the month Artemisius, [Jyar,] a certain prodigious and incredible phenomenon appeared; I suppose the account of it would seem to be a fable, were it not related by those that saw it, and were not the events that followed it of so considerable a nature as to deserve such signals; for, before sun-setting, chariots and troops of soldiers in their armour were seen running about among the clouds, and surrounding of cities. Moreover, at that feast which we call Pentecost, as the priests were going by night into the inner [court of the] temple, as their custom was, to perform their sacred ministrations, they said that, **in the first place, they felt a quaking, and heard a great noise, and after that they heard a sound as of a great multitude, saying, "Let us remove hence."**[46]

Sepher Yosippon also recorded this event.

> When the holiday of Shavu'oth came in those days, during the night the priests heard within the Temple something like the sound of men going and the sound of men marching in a multitude going into the Temple, and a

---

[45] Morais, Daniel. n.d. "The Flight and Return of the Christians, like the Exile and Return of the Jews from Babylon, is an Earthly Reflection of the Resurrection." Revelation Revolution Foundation. Accessed December 9, 2022. https://www.revelationrevolution.org/flight-return-christians-like-exile-return-jews-babylon-earthly-reflection-resurrection.

[46] Josephus, War, 6.5.3.

terrible and mighty voice was heard speaking: "Let's go and leave this House."[47]

These events seem to represent the desired resurrection:

- The ground shook, perhaps indicating bodies coming out of their graves
- Although these bodies were invisible or semi-visible, their voice was heard, which is consistent with the Biblical description of resurrection bodies
- This event occurred two to seven weeks after the vision of angelic armies on the clouds, fulfilling the requirement that the dead rise when Christ returns[48]
- These events appeared in 66 AD, within the disciples' generation, fulfilling the condition that the resurrection was “about to” happen.

It is important to note that the Bible is completely trustworthy, whether the above historical event mentioned or another represents the on-time general resurrection of the dead. As the

---

[47]Yosippon, Mediaeval History, 87.

[48]Josephus said this resurrection-like event happened on Pentecost, 66 AD which would be around June 18 (Sivan 6) according to tables of the Babylonian calendar published in 1971 by Parker and Dubberstein <https://webspace.science.uu.nl/~gent0113/babylon/babycal_converter.htm>. He also said the angelic armies were seen on the clouds "on the one and twentieth day of the month Artemisius, [Jyar,]" which when translated into the Julian calendar is June 4 and puts this exactly two weeks earlier. However, other parallel historical accounts indicate the angelic armies were seen on the same day as other miraculous events that occurred on the last day of Passover, May 5 (Nisan 21) or forty-four days before.

Bible promises a resurrection within the disciples' lifetime, believers can trust that it has already occurred.

Summary

The Bible teaches these three things about the resurrection of the saints:

1. The saints wait in Sheol/Hades until the general resurrection at Christ's return.
2. At the resurrection, they rise in heavenly, spiritual bodies that may or may not be visible.
3. They ascend into heaven, where they remain forever.

A unique event in 66 AD seemed to fulfill this expected resurrection on time, which is good news! Since the resurrection happened as promised in the disciples' lifetime, when Christians die, they no longer go to Sheol or Hades but proceed directly to heaven!

> Revelation 14:13 (NLT) And I heard a voice from heaven saying, "Write this down: Blessed are those who die in the Lord from now on. Yes, says the Spirit, they are blessed indeed, for they will rest from their hard work; for their good deeds follow them!"

Saints have much more hope than before.

> Ecclesiastes 9:5 (ESV) For the living know that they will die, but the dead know nothing, and they have no more reward, for the memory of them is forgotten.

Today, when one trusts Christ as Savior, his future heavenly body is planted as a seed inside him. When his earthly body dies, that seed sprouts, and he instantly enters that heavenly body and is carried up to heaven.

> 1 Corinthians 15:35-38 (ESV) But someone will ask, "How are the dead raised? With what kind of body do they come?" You foolish person! What you sow does not come to life unless it dies. And what you sow is not the body that is to be, but a bare kernel, perhaps of wheat or of some other grain. But God gives it a body as he has chosen, and to each kind of seed its own body.

While heaven was not available to saints who had not been resurrected, believers may take comfort in the fact that the resurrection came to pass as prophesied in the disciples' generation and today believers can enter heaven.

The resurrection can be likened to a store during a super sale, where those who wait in line rush in when the doors open, while those who come later can enter without waiting. Similarly, those who waited in "line" in Hades had their judgment postponed until the resurrection when they could finally enter heaven. Those who died after the resurrection could immediately face judgment and enter without waiting.

By discovering what the scriptures teach about the resurrection, believers can embrace the return of Christ with clarity and confidence. However, one cannot say a resurrection happened without raising questions about the Millennium reign of Christ. The Millennium in Revelation describes two resurrections, one at its beginning and one at its end. How do these two events fit into history?

Chapter 7
Paul's Millennium

The Millennium reign of Christ, described by John in Revelation 20:1-15, is a mysterious passage and sits inside one of the most symbol-driven books of the Bible. The best way to understand scripture is to let scripture interpret scripture. It is interesting to note that nowhere else does the Bible describe a thousand year reign of Christ; however, there are clues in scripture to help the curious reader discover more about it. Several unique events surround the Millennium. At its beginning:

1. Satan is bound (Revelation 20:1-3).

2. Martyrs who hold to the testimony of Jesus and do not accept the mark of the beast are resurrected (Revelation 20:4).

3. Christ reigns supreme for a limited time until his enemies are defeated (Revelation 20:6).
   Note: Christ reigns exclusively for a limited period of time (his Millennial reign), but thereafter reigns jointly with God (Revelation 11:15). Christ's limited, supreme reign under God (the Millennium) resembles the authority of Joseph under Pharaoh (Genesis 41:39-44).

4. Martyrs reign as priests with him (Revelation 20:6).

At the end of the Millennium:

5. Satan is defeated forever (Revelation 20:7,10).

6. A second resurrection takes place which includes the wicked (Revelation 20:11-15).
7. God judges the righteous and wicked (Revelation 20:13).
8. Death is defeated forever (Revelation 20:5,14).
9. The limited, supreme reign of Christ ends (Revelation 20:4), and the reign of God and Christ commences (Revelation 21:3-4,7).

Although the Bible contains no prophetic precedent for a thousand year reign of Christ, it does talk about these notable events, allowing one to estimate when the Millennium takes place.

1 Corinthians 15: The Millennium?

Paul describes all the elements of the end of the Millennium in 1 Corinthians 15.

> 1 Corinthians 15:20-28 (ESV) But in fact Christ has been raised from the dead, the firstfruits of those who have fallen asleep. 21 For as by a man came death, by a man has come also the resurrection of the dead. 22 For as in Adam all die, so also in Christ shall all be made alive. 23 But each in his own order: Christ the firstfruits, then at his coming those who belong to Christ. 24 Then comes the end, when he delivers the kingdom to God the Father after destroying every rule and every authority and power. 25 For he must reign until he has put all his enemies under his feet. 26 The last enemy to be destroyed is death. 27 For "God has put all things in subjection under his [Christ's] feet." But when it says, "all things are put in subjection," it is plain that he

> [God] is excepted who put all things in subjection under him [Christ]. 28 When all things are subjected to him [Christ], then the Son himself will also be subjected to him [God] who put all things in subjection under him [Christ], that God may be all in all.

Similar to John's description in Revelation of the end of the Millennium, Paul has just described:

1. The destruction of death: “The last enemy to be destroyed is death” (1 Corinthians 15:26).
2. The destruction of all Christ's enemies, which would include Satan: “For he must reign until he has put all his enemies under his feet” (1 Corinthians 15:25-26).
3. The second resurrection: “For as by a man came death, by a man has come also the resurrection of the dead. 22 For as in Adam all die, so also in Christ shall all be made alive” (1 Corinthians 15:21-22).
4. The ending of Christ's supreme reign: “When all things are subjected to him [Christ], then the Son himself will also be subjected to him [God]” (1 Corinthians 15:28).

Paul says that Christ must reign until his enemies are under his feet.

> 1 Corinthians 15:25 (ESV) For he must reign **until he has put all his enemies under his feet**.

The reign Paul describes began when Christ ascended into heaven and sat at the right hand of God.

Hebrews 10:12-13 (ESV) But when Christ had offered for all time a single sacrifice for sins, he sat down at the right hand of God, 13 **waiting from that time until his enemies should be made a footstool for his feet.**

1 Peter 3:21-22 (ESV) ...through the resurrection of Jesus Christ, 22 who has gone into heaven and is at the right hand of God, with angels, authorities, and powers having been subjected to him.

Revelation 3:21 (ESV) The one who conquers, I will grant him to sit with me on my throne, as I also conquered and sat down with my Father on his throne.

See also Ephesians 1:20-23; Hebrews 1:3-4,13; 2:8.

Could the ascension of Christ be the start of the Millennium? Surprisingly, around the time of Christ's ascension, the events that marked the beginning of the Millennium also occurred.

1. Satan was bound during Jesus' ministry (Matthew 12:28-29; Luke 10:17-20; John 12:31-32; Jude 6).
2. Holy saints came out of their graves with Jesus at his resurrection (Matthew 27:51-53).
3. Christ began his supreme reign for a limited time at God's right hand until his enemies were defeated (1 Corinthians 15:25; Ephesians 1:20-23; Hebrews 1:3-4,13; 2:8; 10:12-13; 1 Peter 3:21-22; Revelation 3:21).
4. Resurrected saints ascended with Christ into heaven (Ephesians 4:8-10; Hebrews 12:1).
5. Christians were called priests (1 Peter 2:5,9-10; Revelation 1:5-6; 5:10).

If Paul describes a supreme reign of Christ in heaven that begins with all the elements of the Millennium and ends with all the elements of the Millennium, it seems probable that he describes the same reign John does.

However, some scholars may doubt this connection. To prove that Paul is describing the Millennium, the following questions will be addressed.

1. Does 1 Corinthians 15 describe the second resurrection or the first?
2. Is Christ supposed to reign from heaven or earth during the Millennium?
3. If "the beast" was an end-time tyrant, how did the saints resurrected with Jesus avoid his mark or die for their testimony of Jesus?
4. How was Satan bound during Paul's ministry if he seemed to still be at work?

If all these questions can be sufficiently answered, then it stands that Paul is describing the Millennium, a reign that had already begun at Christ's ascension.

1 Corinthians 15: The Second Resurrection

Does 1 Corinthians 15 describe the second resurrection or the first?

The Millennium has two resurrections, one at its beginning and one at its end. In Revelation, death is defeated at the second resurrection at the end of the Millennium, not the first resurrection at the beginning.

> Revelation 20:13-14 (ESV) And the sea gave up the dead who were in it, Death and Hades gave up the dead who were in them, and they were judged, each one of them, according to what they had done. 14 **Then Death and Hades were thrown into the lake of fire**. This is the second death, the lake of fire.

In 1 Corinthians 15:52-55, it can be deduced that Paul describes the second resurrection, because he says that death is defeated at the moment of the resurrection.

> 1 Corinthians 15:52-55 (ESV) in a moment, in the twinkling of an eye, at the last trumpet. For the trumpet will sound, and the dead will be raised imperishable, and we shall be changed. 53 For this perishable body must put on the imperishable, and this mortal body must put on immortality. 54 When the perishable puts on the imperishable, and the mortal puts on immortality, then shall come to pass the saying that is written: "**Death is swallowed up in victory**." 55 "O death, where is your victory? O death, where is your sting?"

As shown, the resurrection of 1 Corinthians 15 accompanies "death swallowed up in victory," proof positive that it is the second resurrection.

Christ Reigns From Where?

Is Christ supposed to reign from heaven or earth during the Millennium?

Most Christians assume Christ returns to earth and reigns from here during the Millennium; however, Revelation does not specify the location of Christ during his reign.

Remember that Christ's enemies and death are destroyed at the end of the Millennium.

> Revelation 20:7,14 (ESV) And when the thousand years are ended, Satan will be released from his prison... 14 Then Death and Hades were thrown into the lake of fire. This is the second death, the lake of fire.

Christ reigns from heaven, not earth, during the Millennium because Paul says Christ does not return to earth until the end of his reign when death is defeated.

> 1 Corinthians 15:23-26 (ESV) "...**then at his coming**... **comes the end**, when he delivers the kingdom to God the Father after destroying every rule and every authority and power. For he must reign **until he has put all his enemies under his feet. The last enemy to be destroyed is death**."

Still, some argue that Christ's return marks the "beginning of the end" and not the "end of the end" of the millennial reign.

However, Christ would not return to begin a reign that had already begun; therefore, he was going to return at the end of his reign. Hebrews says Christ's reign had already begun at his ascension, and he was currently waiting in heaven for his enemies to be made a footstool for his feet.

> Hebrews 10:12-13 (ESV) But when Christ had offered for all time a single sacrifice for sins, he sat down at the right

hand of God, 13 waiting from that time until his enemies should be made a footstool for his feet.

In Paul's first letter to the Corinthians, he stated that the moment that Christ returns is the end.

1 Corinthians 1:8 (ESV) ...who will sustain you **to the end**, guiltless **in the day of our Lord Jesus Christ**.

Christ returns the day death is defeated. Therefore, he reigns from heaven at God's right hand during the Millennium.

Matthew 27: The First Resurrection

Jesus' resurrection is described as the first resurrection (Acts 26:23; 1 Corinthians 15:20; Colossians 1:18) and happens simultaneously with the resurrection of the saints in Jerusalem.

Matthew 27:51-53 (ESV) And behold, the curtain of the temple was torn in two, from top to bottom. And the earth shook, and the rocks were split. 52 The tombs also were opened. And many bodies of the saints who had fallen asleep were raised, 53 and coming out of the tombs after his resurrection they went into the holy city and appeared to many.

The first resurrection includes only those who have been "beheaded for the testimony of Jesus" and have not "worshiped the beast" (Revelation 20:4). Matthew's account of resurrection consists of the bodies of the saints who had fallen asleep. Revelation 20:4 and Matthew 27:52 seem to point to the same martyred saints, those who were part of the first resurrection with Christ.

Avoiding the Mark

"If 'the beast' was an end-time tyrant, how did the saints resurrected with Jesus avoid his mark or die for their testimony of Jesus?"

Jesus states that the Law, Prophets, and Psalms "testify" about himself.

> Luke 24:44 (ESV) Then he said to them, "These are my words that I spoke to you while I was still with you, that everything **written about me** in the Law of Moses and the Prophets and the Psalms must be fulfilled."

> John 5:39 (ESV) You search **the Scriptures** because you think that in them you have eternal life; and it is they that **bear witness about me**

> John 5:46 (ESV) For if you believed Moses, you would believe me; **for he wrote of me**.

The Old Testament prophets were martyred for holding this testimony of Christ.

> Matthew 23:29-32 (ESV) "Woe to you, scribes and Pharisees, hypocrites! For you build the tombs of the prophets and decorate the monuments of the righteous, saying, 'If we had lived in the days of our fathers, we would not have taken part with them in shedding the blood of the prophets.' Thus you witness against yourselves that you are sons of those who murdered the prophets. Fill up, then, the measure of your fathers.

In his presentation to the Berean Bible Church, researcher and speaker Robert Cruickshank argued that the tombs of the martyred prophets that the Pharisees would decorate were the same ones opened at Jesus' resurrection (Matthew 27:51-53).[49]

Hebrews says that Moses considered the "reproach of Christ" to be "greater wealth than the treasures of Egypt" (Hebrews 11:26 [ESV]), showing that even Old Testament saints could be persecuted for their faith in Jesus.

To receive the beast's mark on the forehead or hand was to forsake the faith in the Messiah and obey the commands of the beast. Revelation says that this beast also lived in the past.

> Revelation 17:8 (ESV) **The beast that you saw was**, and is not, and is about to rise from the bottomless pit and go to destruction.

In the article "Revelation, the Mark of the Beast," Cruickshank quotes Richard W. Engle, who believes that the beast was greater than a symbol for Rome/Nero. It "became a symbol for great kings and empires who punished Israel or whom Israel should avoid."[50] Egypt/Pharaoh (Ezekiel 29:2-3) and Babylon/ Nebuchadnezzar (Jeremiah 51:34) were called "serpents" or "beasts" towards God's people, and they tormented those who held to the testimony of the Messiah. In Psalm 74, David prophetically calls for God's help at a time of foreign occupation (likely the Jews exile to Babylon), reminding God

---

[49] Cruickshank, Robert. 2022. "The First Resurrection (Rev. 20:4-5) - Bob Cruickshank Jr (2022 Conference)." YouTube. https://youtu.be/46hrjwTbHMc?t=655.

[50] Cruickshank, Robert. 2022. "Guest Article: Revelation, the Mark of the Beast- Part 1- By Robert ..." Preterist Research Institute. https://bibleprophecy.com/articles/2022/06/25/guest-article-revelation-the-mark-of-the-beast-part-1-by-robert-cruickshank/.

that he had slain the Leviathan, or foreign persecutors, in their past (Psalm 74:14).

The Christian Jews would naturally contrast receiving the mark of the beast "on their foreheads or their hands" with not serving God's laws or holding faithfully to their testimony about Christ (Exodus 13:9; Deuteronomy 6:4-8; Revelation 14:11-12). See “Chapter 14 A Dramatic End” for a more thorough explanation.

Matthew 27, Ezekiel 37, and Revelation

In an unpublished manuscript, Cruickshank points out that Matthew 27:51-53 is strikingly similar to Ezekiel 37:1-4,[51] prophesying about a resurrection of Israel. Ezekiel 37-48 also correlates with Revelation 20-22.[52]

Matthew and Ezekiel both:

- include the Spirit raising the bodies of many holy people (Ezekiel 37:2,11; Matthew 27:52)
- have an earthquake (Ezekiel 37:7; Matthew 27:51)
- include opened tombs or graves (Ezekiel 37:12; Matthew 27:52)
- involve leading the resurrected into the Holy City afterward (Ezekiel 37:12; Matthew 27:53)

---

[51] Cruickshank, Unpublished Manuscript, 76-83.

[52] Cruickshank, Unpublished Manuscript, 87.

Ezekiel 37-48 and Revelation 20-22 also seem to prophesy about the same events.

Ezekiel	**Revelation**
37:10 - Revival of dry bones	First resurrection (20:5)
37:21 - Reunited kingdom	Saints rule for one thousand years (20:4)
38:2 - Gog and Magog battle	Gog and Magog battle (20:8)
39:4 - Gorging of the birds	Gorging of the birds (19:21)
40:2 - Taken to a high mountain	Taken to a high mountain (21:10)
40:5 - Temple is measured	City is measured (21:15)
43:2 - Temple full of God's	City full of God's glory (21:23)
47:12a - River of life	River of life (22:1)
47:12b - Trees with healing leaves	Tree with healing leaves (22:2)

If A = B and B = C, then A = C. If Matthew correlates with Ezekiel and if Ezekiel relates to Revelation, then these striking similarities suggest Matthew 27 and Revelation 20 may describe the same first resurrection of the Millennium.

Martyrs Reigned with Christ

The saints resurrected in Matthew 27:51-53 ascended to heaven with Jesus and were reigning as priests with him.

If Christ began his reign when he entered heaven, these saints likely also began their reign when they entered heaven with him. Peter and John considered all Christians to be priests (1 Peter 2:5,9-10; Revelation 1:5-6; 5:10).

Paul tells the Ephesians that Christ took captives with him when he ascended into heaven. It is apparent these were the saints who rose with him at his resurrection.

> Ephesians 4:8-9 (NIV) "When he ascended on high, he took many captives and gave gifts to his people."
>
> 9 (What does "he ascended" mean except that he also descended to the lower, earthly regions? 10 He who descended is the very one who ascended higher than all the heavens, in order to fill the whole universe.)

Early church father Eusebius says that the saints who rose with Jesus were taken to heaven with him.

> Thus, too, His own body was raised up, and many bodies of the sleeping saints arose, and came together with Him into the holy and real City of Heaven, as rightly is said by the holy words: "Death has prevailed and swallowed men up"; and again: "The Lord God has taken away every tear from every face."[53]

Some non-Biblical writings such as the Gospel of Nicodemus, Vol 8, Chapter 1 and the Archko Volume state that thousands rose with Jesus from the grave and ascended into the clouds.[54]

---

53 Eusebius, Demonstratio Evangelica, 4.12.186, http://www.intratext.com/IXT/ENG0882/_P1B.HTM.

54 "Thousands rose from the dead with Jesus on Easter." n.d. Bible Probe. Accessed December 9, 2022. http://www.bibleprobe.com/descent.htm.

Perhaps this is why Hebrews says a "great cloud of witnesses" surrounds the first century believers (Hebrews 12:1), and they have come "to the assembly of the firstborn who are enrolled in heaven" (Hebrews 12:23 [ESV]). Perhaps these were the same witnesses given authority to judge (Revelation 20:4).

Jesus Bound Satan

Around the time of Christ's ascension, during Jesus' ministry, Satan was bound. In one place, Jesus metaphorically described how he had bound Satan.

> Matthew 12:28-29 (NIV) But if it is by the Spirit of God that I drive out demons, then the kingdom of God has come upon you. "Or again, how can anyone enter a strong man's house and carry off his possessions unless he first ties up the strong man? Then he can plunder his house.

Jesus saw Satan fall like lightning from heaven and gave his disciples authority over all demons (Luke 10:17-20). He told them when he would go to the cross, "the ruler of this world will be cast out" (John 12:31-32). Jude, writing after Christ's ascension, states:

> Jude 6 (NIV) And the angels who did not keep their positions of authority but abandoned their proper dwelling —these he has kept in darkness, bound with everlasting chains for judgment on the great Day.

Demons were presently imprisoned and waiting for the great judgment on the day of Christ's return. Perhaps these included demons Christ bound during his ministry?

Cruickshank believes Satan was bound during Jesus' testing in the wilderness when Jesus said, "Be gone, Satan!" (Matthew 4:10). In his sermon delivered at Berean Bible Church, he connected this binding with the binding of Satan in Revelation 20.[55]

Nicodemus and Satan's Binding

The Gospel of Nicodemus, a non-Biblical writing, says Christ descended into Hades and ordered Satan to be bound in Hades until his second appearance.

> Then the King of glory seized the chief satrap Satan by the head, and delivered him to His angels, and said: With iron chains bind his hands and his feet, and his neck, and his mouth. Then He delivered him to Hades, and said: Take him, and keep him secure till my second appearing.[56]

Although non-canonical writings do not hold the same credibility or authority as inspired scripture, this demonstrates one view in the early church and supports the theory that Jesus bound Satan at the cross.

Satan’s Limits

How was Satan bound during the Millennium if he seemed to still be at work?

---

55 Cruickshank, Robert. 2022. "The Binding of Satan in the Gospels - Bob Cruickshank Jr (2022 Conference)." YouTube. https://www.youtube.com/watch?v=qSGjNP-S2n0.

56 Kirby, Peter. n.d. "Gospel of Nicodemus: The Descent of Christ into Hell (ANF text)." Early Christian Writings. Accessed December 9, 2022. http://www.earlychristianwritings.com/text/gospelnicodemus-roberts2.html.

Satan may have blinded the minds of unbelievers (Mark 4:15; 2 Corinthians 4:4), but he was prevented from bringing nations to war against Christianity.

> Revelation 20:3 (BLB) And he cast him into the Abyss, and shut and sealed it over him, **so that he should not deceive the nations any longer**, until the thousand years were completed. After these things it is necessary for him to be released for a little time.

Satan will be eager to do whatever he was prevented from doing once he is released. As soon as he is released, he gathers the nations of Gog and Magog together and deceives them to wage war against the saints.

> Revelation 20:7-9 (ESV) And **when the thousand years are ended, Satan will be released from his prison** and will come out to **deceive the nations** that are at the four corners of the earth, Gog and Magog, to **gather them for battle**; their number is like the sand of the sea. And they marched up over the broad plain of the earth **and surrounded the camp of the saints** and the beloved city...

This binding was reminiscent of Satan's limitations in persecuting Job.

> Job 1:8-12 (NIV) Then the Lord said to Satan, "Have you considered my servant Job? There is no one on earth like him; he is blameless and upright, a man who fears God and shuns evil."
>
> 9 "Does Job fear God for nothing?" Satan replied. 10 "Have you not put a hedge around him and his household and everything he has? You have blessed the work of his hands, so that his flocks and herds are spread throughout the land.

> 11 But now stretch out your hand and strike everything he has, and he will surely curse you to your face."
>
> 12 The Lord said to Satan, "Very well, then, everything he has is in your power, **but on the man himself do not lay a finger**."

Satan was permitted to make life uncomfortable for Job, to take his possessions, but not to harm Job himself. Perhaps similarly, Satan could persecute the saints for several years but not wipe them out under a state-sponsored genocide.

The Romans and Jews tolerated Christians for thirty to forty years, from Pentecost until around April 62 AD (the Millennium period). Emperor Tiberius had ordered Roman officials not to interfere with the new religion and even tried to legalize Christianity.[57]

However, around 62-64 AD, with the help of apostate Jews the full force of the Roman state was brought against Christianity. Unbelieving Jews killed James, expelled Christians from Jerusalem, and likely encouraged Caesar Nero to blame the fire of Rome on Christians. This persecution may well be the fulfillment of Jesus' prophecy of the Great Tribulation and persecution of the elect (Matthew 24:22). Historical fulfillments of Revelation are explored in "Chapter 11 The Millennium End."

---

[57] Constitutional Rights Foundation. n.d. "Constitutional Rights Foundation." Constitutional Rights Foundation. Accessed January 6, 2023. https://www.crf-usa.org/bill-of-rights-in-action/bria-13-4-b-religious-tolerance-and-persecution-in-the-roman-empire.

Though one must accept that Satan could still cause trouble, God prevented him from making war against Christianity until the end of the Millennium.

Summary

To establish that the Millennium of Revelation and the supreme reign of Christ in 1 Corinthians 15 are the same, four conflicting issues were resolved.

1. Paul describes the second resurrection in 1 Corinthians 15 when he says that death will be defeated at this resurrection.
2. Christ reigns from heaven, not earth, during the Millennium because Paul says Christ does not return to earth until the end of his reign.
3. The beast existed in the Old Testament, and the saints who were faithful to the testimony of the Messiah in scripture avoided his mark.
4. Satan was not limited from all troublemaking, but was bound from bringing nations to war against Christians.

With these issues resolved, it is clear that Paul and Revelation both describe the same reality; Paul describes the Millennium in a literal fashion, while John employs the use of symbolism in the book of Revelation.

In each narrative, at the beginning of Christ's Millennial reign:

1. Satan is bound (Revelation 20:1-3; Matthew 12:28-29; Luke 10:17-20; John 12:31-32; Jude 6).

2. The faithful martyrs rise (Revelation 20:4; Matthew 27:51-53).

3. Christ reigns supreme for a limited time until his enemies are defeated (Revelation 20:6-10; 1 Corinthians 15:20-28; Ephesians 1:20-23; Hebrews 1:3-4,13; 2:8; 10:12-13).

4. The resurrected martyrs reign with him (Revelation 20:4; Ephesians 4:8-10) as priests (Revelation 20:6; 1 Peter 2:5,9-10; Revelation 1:5-6; 5:10).

At the end of Paul and John's reign:

1. Death is defeated forever (Revelation 20:5,14; 1 Corinthians 15:20-28).

2. Satan is defeated forever (Revelation 20:7,10; 1 Corinthians 15:20-28).

3. The final resurrection is finished (Revelation 20:11-15; Acts 24:15; 1 Corinthians 15:20-28).

4. The supreme reign of Christ ends (Revelation 20:4) and God and Christ's reign are established (Revelation 21:3-4,7; 1 Corinthians 15:20-28).

With these facts, it is sensible to conclude that the Millennial reign began at Christ's ascension and was present during Paul's ministry.

Though it may seem odd for John to write about a Millennium that had already begun in a prophecy about the future, remember that the angel explicitly instructed him to write about the things he had seen.

> Revelation 1:9 (ESV) Write therefore the things that **you have seen**, those that are and those that are to take place after this.

John was not just telling a prophecy but a story that was still progressing at the time of his writing. Several examples of this could be given. Most scholars agree that when John spoke about the woman giving birth and the dragon trying to snatch her baby away (Revelation 12), it was describing the birth of Jesus, which would have been past from the writing of Revelation. When the angel said that the seven heads of the beast were seven kings, he explained that five of these kings had already fallen (Revelation 17:10).

John was telling the same story as Paul. Christ had ascended into heaven and was currently reigning at the right hand of God.

Chapter 8
The Millennium's Approaching End

The previous chapter demonstrated that the Millennium began with Christ's ascension into heaven. But when would it end? In 1030 AD, which is a literal thousand years? Or is it still happening today?

Many scholars recognize that John's thousand years was a symbolic number. Is this true? The reader should notice that the events expected to occur at the end of the thousand years were all promised a soon fulfillment.

Bible Uses Hyperbole

Logically, one might think the Millennium represents one thousand literal years, or at least a very long period of time.

Most would hesitate to imagine it could mean a much shorter time span, say thirty to forty years.

However, the Bible frequently uses hyperbole to emphasize the greatness of an act, even if it is technically exaggerated. Nations surrounding Israel used hyperbolic numbers to glorify their kings, so the Israelites did the same to glorify God.

> 1 Kings 20:30 (ESV) The rest of them escaped to the city of Aphek, **where the wall collapsed on twenty-seven thousand of them.**

> 1 Kings 8:63 (ESV) Solomon offered a sacrifice of fellowship offerings to the Lord: **twenty-two thousand cattle** and **a**

> **hundred and twenty thousand sheep and goats**. So the king and all the Israelites dedicated the temple of the Lord.

These are just two examples of exaggeration, or hyperbole, used many times in the scripture, especially in the Old Testament. In a sermon to the Berean Bible Church, Cruickshank gave many other clear examples of hyperbole in scripture.[58]

However, this begs the question, why did John state Christ's reign would be a thousand years if it should not be taken literally?

Why Say a Thousand Years?

Jewish Rabbis and Christians living in Jesus' time believed the world was divided into seven figurative millennia corresponding to the seven days of creation. The Messianic age was the sixth millennia (Genesis 2:2-3; Psalm 90:4; Hebrews 4:8-11) and when God's kingdom arrived, it would mark the beginning of the seventh millennium or "cosmic Sabbath," an eternal period. The early church father Irenaeus, writing in 175-185 AD, says,

> For in as many days as this world was made, in so many thousand years shall it be concluded. And for this reason the Scripture says: Thus the heaven and the earth were finished, and all their adornment. And God brought to a conclusion upon the sixth day the works that He had made;

---

[58] Cruickshank, Robert. 2021. "The Millennium: Significance of the Thousand Year Symbol (Rev 20:1-10)." YouTube. https://www.youtube.com/watch?v=wR9GWpSGyBU.

> and God rested upon the seventh day from all His works. Genesis 2:2 This is an account of the things formerly created, as also it is a prophecy of what is to come. For the day of the Lord is as a thousand years; 2 Peter 3:8 and in six days created things were completed: it is evident, therefore, that they will come to an end at the sixth thousand year.[59]

> ...These are [to take place] in the times of the kingdom, that is, upon the seventh day, which has been sanctified, in which God rested from all the works which He created, which is the true Sabbath of the righteous[60]

A thousand years referred to the entire length of each age, and some scholars argued that the sixth millennia would last much less than a thousand years. They called these days the "days of the Messiah" and expected them to be a transition period between the former ages and the eternal age to come. Edward E. Stevens, in his unpublished PDF "What the Rabbis Said about the Millennium" noticed that some Jewish scholars in the first century even argued this eon would last only forty years. Stevens quotes Abraham Cohen's work:

> Many Rabbis believed that the period of the Messiah was to be only a transitory stage between this world and the World to Come, and opinions differed on its duration. "How long will the days of the Messiah last?"

---

[59]Irenaeus, Against Heresies, 5.28.3, http://www.newadvent.org/fathers/0103528.htm.

[60]Irenaeus, Against Heresies, 5.33.2, http://www.newadvent.org/fathers/0103533.htm.

R. Akiba [c. 120-140 AD] said, "Forty years, as long as the Israelites were in the wilderness."

R. Eliezer (b. Jos) said, "A hundred years."

R. Berechya said in the name of R. Dosa, "Six hundred years."

R. Judah the Prince said, "Four hundred years, as long as the Israelites were in Egypt."

R. Eliezer (b. Hyrcanus) [c. 80-120 AD] said, "A thousand years." R. Abbahu said, "Seven thousand years."

...

Other versions read:

R. Eliezer [c. 80-120 AD] said, "The days of the Messiah will be forty years."

R. Eleazar b. Azariah said, Seventy years.

...

R. Eliezer said, The days of the Messiah will be forty years.

...

It was taught in the School of Elijah, The world will endure six thousand years — two thousand years in chaos (from Creation to the Revelation at Sinai), two thousand with Torah, and two thousand years will be the days of the Messiah (Sanh. 97a).[61]

Most considered it to be a time of great anguish.

---

[61]Cohen, Abraham. 1949. Everyman's Talmud with an introduction. New American ed. New York, NY: E.P. Dutton, 356.

> B. F. Westcott (1889). Jewish teachers distinguished a 'present age' (this age) from 'that age' (the age to come). Between 'the present age' of imperfection and conflict and trial and 'the age to come' of the perfect reign of God they placed 'the days of the Messiah,' which they sometimes reckoned in the former, sometimes in the latter, and sometimes distinct from both. **They were, however, commonly agreed that the passage from one age to the other would be through a period of intense sorrow and anguish, 'the travail-pains' of the new birth (Mt. 24:8).** The apostolic writers, fully conscious of the spiritual crisis through which they were passing[,] speak of their own time as the 'last days' (Acts 2:17; James 5:3; comp. 2 Tim. 3:1); the 'last hour' (1 John. 2:18); the 'end of the times' (1 Peter 1:20; 2 Pet. 3:3); 'the last time' (Jude 18).[62]

First-century Christians would have been familiar with these concepts, which would have colored their understanding of the symbols in Revelation. If one places himself in the shoes of those to whom John addressed his letter, one finds the Millennium may describe the "days of the Messiah," the sixth millennium, days that scholars predicted could last forty years.

Besides the symbolic nature of the "thousand year reign," it should be noted that the end of the Millennium was expected soon. Four universe-changing and unrepeatable events happen at its end.

---

[62]Westcott, Brooke F. 1903. The Epistle to the Hebrews. Third Edition ed. New York: The Macmillan Company. https://biblicalstudies.org.uk/pdf/e-books/westcott_b-f/hebrews_westcott.pdf, 6.

1. Heaven casts Satan into the lake of fire (Revelation 20:7,10).
2. Death is thrown into the lake of fire (Revelation 20:14).
3. God resurrects the wicked dead (Revelation 20:5,11-14).
4. God judges the dead (Revelation 20:5,11-14).

One can reason that if these events happen only once, whenever the Bible talks about them, it describes the end of the Millennium. The Bible says these four events will come about shortly, without delay, at Christ's return.

Satan Crushed

Paul explicitly says that Satan would soon be destroyed.

> Romans 16:20 (ESV) The God of peace will soon crush Satan under your feet.

He alludes to the prophecy in Genesis concerning Satan's final defeat:

> Genesis 3:15 (Berean Standard Bible) And I will put enmity between you and the woman, and between your seed and her seed. He will crush your head, and you will strike his heel."

The "Seed," referring to Christ, would finally crush Satan under his feet. Death and Satan are defeated at Christ's coming.

> 1 Corinthians 15:21-26 (ESV) For as by a man came death, by a man has come also the resurrection of the dead. 22 For as in Adam all die, so also in Christ shall all be made alive. 23 But each in his own order: Christ the firstfruits, **then at**

> **his coming** those who belong to Christ. 24 **Then comes the end**, when he delivers the kingdom to God the Father **after destroying every rule and every authority and power**. 25 For he must reign until he has put **all his enemies under his feet**. 26 **The last enemy to be destroyed is death.**

Satan is the ultimate of all Christ's enemies and would be defeated when Christ returned.

Christ's Return Ends the Millennium

Every time the New Testament says Christ will return soon, it is saying the end of the Millennium is soon. Remember that in the previous chapter, "Chapter 7 Paul's Millennium" in the section "Christ Reigns From Where?" it was shown that Christ would not return at the beginning of the Millennium but at its end. Hence, a soon return was a soon end to the Millennium.

The Resurrection of the Wicked

Revelation describes two resurrections, one at the beginning and one at the end of the Millennium. Only the second resurrection includes the wicked dead (Revelation 20:11-15) while only the righteous rise in the first resurrection (Revelation 20:4). If one knows the timing of the resurrection of the wicked, he discovers when the Millennium will end.

Paul explicitly said the unrighteous were about to be resurrected when Christ returned.

> Acts 24:15 (LSV) having hope toward God, which they themselves also wait for, **[that] there is about to be a**

resurrection of the dead, both of righteous and unrighteous;

2 Timothy 4:1 (LSV) I fully testify, then, before God, and the Lord Jesus Christ, **who is about to judge [the] living and dead at His appearing** and His Kingdom

As the end of all things drew near, Peter said God was ready to judge both the living and the dead, including the wicked or those who "maligned" the Christians.

1 Peter 4:4-7 (ESV) **With respect to this they are surprised when you do not join them in the same flood of debauchery, and they malign you; 5 but they will give account to him who is ready to judge the living and the dead.** 6 For this is why the gospel was preached even to those who are dead, that though judged in the flesh the way people are, they might live in the spirit the way God does. 7 **The end of all things is at hand**; therefore be self-controlled and sober-minded for the sake of your prayers.

Daniel's Resurrection of the Wicked

Jesus promised his disciples that the resurrection of the wicked dead, spoken of in Daniel, would occur in his generation. Daniel prophesied that at a time of unprecedented distress, the wicked dead would be resurrected.

Daniel 12:1-2 (ESV) At that time shall arise Michael, the great prince who has charge of your people. **And there shall be a time of trouble, such as never has been since there was a nation till that time**. But at that time your people shall be delivered, everyone whose name shall be found **written in the book**. 2 And **many of those who sleep**

However, each uses nearly identical language, contains an element that can only happen once, and is promised soon.

The three judgment passages have nearly identical language.

Matthew 16 Son of Man Judgment	Matthew 25 Sheep and Goats Judgment	Revelation 20 Great White Throne Judgment
For the Son of Man is about to come in the glory His Father... (Matthew 16:27)	When the Son of Man comes in his glory, and all the angels with him, then he will sit on his glorious throne (Matthew 25:31)	Then I saw a great white throne and him who was seated on it. (Revelation 20:11)
with His angels (Matthew 16:27)	and all the angels with him (Matthew 25:31)	And the armies of heaven, arrayed in fine linen, white and pure, were following him on white horses (Revelation 19:14)

the Son of Man coming in His kingdom (Matthew 16:28)	Then the King will say to those on his right, 'Come, you who are blessed by my Father, inherit the kingdom prepared for you from the foundation of the world.' (Matthew 25:34)	The one who conquers will have this heritage (Revelation 21:7)
and then He will give to each according to his deeds (Matthew 16:27)	Before him will be gathered all the nations, and he will separate people one from another as a shepherd separates the sheep from the goats. (Matthew 25:32)	And I saw the dead, great and small, standing before the throne, and books were opened. Then another book was opened, which is the book of life. And the dead were judged by what was written in the books, according to what they had

and then He will give to each according to his deeds (Matthew 16:27)	"Then he will say to those on his left, 'Depart from me, you cursed, into the eternal fire prepared for the devil and his angels.'" (Matthew 25:41)	And if anyone's name was not found written in the book of life, he was thrown into the lake of fire (Revelation 20:15) (Compare to Revelation 20:10 where the Devil was thrown into
there are some of those standing here who shall not taste of death until they have seen the Son of Man coming in His kingdom (Matthew 16:28)	Watch therefore, for you know neither the day nor the hour (Matthew 25:13). Be always on the watch, and pray that you may be able to escape all that is about to happen, and that you may be able to stand before the Son of Man. (Luke 21:36)	Shortly to come to pass (Rev. 1:1,3;3:10-11;22:6-7,10,12,20) with no delay at the sounding of the seventh trumpet (Revelation 10:5-7)

The similarity in language of these three judgments strongly indicates that they are speaking of the same event, the very same judgment.

The Established Kingdom

Each judgment passage above described the arrival of the kingdom of heaven (Matthew 16:28 and its parallel Mark 9:1; Matthew 25:34; Revelation 21:7).

> Matthew 16:28 (BLB) there are some of those standing here who shall not taste of death until they have seen the Son of Man **coming in His kingdom**

> Matthew 25:34 (ESV) Then the King will say to those on his right, 'Come, you who are blessed by my Father, **inherit the kingdom prepared for you from the foundation of the world.**'

> Revelation 21:7 (ESV) The one who conquers will have **this heritage**

Daniel prophesied that the kingdom of heaven would arrive only once and remain forever.

> Daniel 2:44 (BSB) In the days of those kings, the God of heaven will set up a kingdom that will never be destroyed, nor will it be left to another people. It will shatter all these kingdoms and bring them to an end, but will itself stand forever.

For something to be established and remain forever, it cannot be re-established. If all three of these passages described the arrival of the kingdom of heaven, they cannot describe separate judgments.

Three Imminent Judgments

Suppose these passages describe separate judgments. Even so, each was promised to occur soon.

The Son of Man Judgment

Only some disciples would die before seeing the Son of Man's Judgment.

> Matthew 16:27-28 (GNT) **For the Son of Man is about to come** in the glory of his Father with his angels, and then he will reward each one according to his deeds. I assure you that **there are some here who will not die until they have seen the Son of Man come as King.**

The Sheep and Goats Judgment

The Sheep and Goats Judgment (Matthew 25:31-46) was promised to occur soon in its parallel passage, Luke 21:34-36.

> Luke 21:34-36 (NIV) "Be careful, or your hearts will be weighed down with carousing, drunkenness and the anxieties of life, and **that day will close on you suddenly like a trap**. 35 For it will come on all those who live on the face of the whole earth. 36 Be always on the **watch**, and pray that you may be able to escape all that **is about to happen**, and that you may be able **to stand before the Son of Man**."

The "day" that was "about to" close on them at an unknown time was the return of the Son of Man to judge the Sheep and Goats (Matthew 24:37,39,42,44,46; 25:31-46).

When reading Luke 21:33 and Matthew 24:35 and following (which contains the Sheep and Goats Judgment), it is clear both passages are parallel and contain similar language.

After Jesus said his generation would not pass until everything was complete (Luke 21:32-33; Matthew 24:34-35), he emphasized the importance of being watchful so that his return would not surprise them (Luke 21:34-36; Matthew 24:36-25:31-46). Just like Noah and the ark, they were to watch for the rains so they could quickly enter the ark to avoid the flood (Matthew 24:37-39) and not be trapped in the coming destruction.

> Matthew 25:13 (ESV) **Watch** therefore, for you know neither the day nor the hour.

Likewise Luke said,

> Luke 21:36 (NIV) Be always on the **watch**, and pray that you may be **able to escape** all that **is about to happen**

Since Luke mentioned that the Son of Man's return in judgment was "about" to happen, the Sheep and Goats Judgment was promised soon.

The Great White Throne Judgment

In the below verse, the angel said that when the seventh trumpet sounded, the mystery of God would be accomplished. He swore an oath that the accomplishment of this mystery since the time it was announced to the prophets would no longer be delayed.

> Revelation 10:5-7 (NIV) Then the angel I had seen standing on the sea and on the land raised his right hand to heaven. 6 And he **swore** by him who lives for ever and ever, who created the heavens and all that is in them, the earth and all that is in it, and the sea and all that is in it, and said, "**There will be no more delay!** 7 But in the days when the seventh angel is about to sound his trumpet, the mystery of God will be accomplished, just as he announced to his servants the prophets.

The seventh or last trumpet is associated with the Great White Throne Judgment, which is where the dead rise (Revelation 20:13), death is defeated forever (Revelation 20:14), and the kingdom of heaven is delivered to the saints (Revelation 21:7). Likewise, at the sounding of the seventh or last trumpet, the dead rise (Revelation 11:18), death is defeated forever (1 Corinthians 15:51-55), and the kingdom of heaven is delivered to God (1 Corinthians 15:24-27; Revelation 11:15,17). This event was imminent and could not be delayed any longer.

It is important to note that Revelation is a cyclical book with repeating elements and was written in an apocalyptic form. Therefore, it should not be interpreted linearly. In similar manner, Revelation has many other instances of repetition:

- the flattening of every island and mountain twice (Revelation 6:14; 16:20),
- the turning of water to blood twice (Revelation 8:9-11; 16:3-6),
- stars falling to earth three times (Revelation 6:13; 8:12; 12:4),

- mounted troops from the Euphrates gathering for battle twice (Revelation 9:14-16; 16:12-16),
- John falling at the angel's feet to worship him and being rebuked twice (Revelation 19:10; 22:8-9),
- the wicked dead being resurrected and judged twice (Revelation 11:18; 20:11-15),
- the marriage of the lamb taking place twice (Revelation 19:6-9; 21:2,9-10),
- and God wiping away every tear from the saints' eyes and them never thirsting again and receiving water from the springs of life twice (Revelation 7:14-17; 21:4,6-7).

The universe-changing events of the seventh trumpet are repeated in the Great White Throne Judgment. These two depictions of the end describe the same event.

According to Deuteronomy 23:21-23, delay in fulfilling an oath is considered a sin, and God cannot sin. Clearly, the seventh trumpet and the Great White Throne Judgment would happen soon.

Summary

Although there is no prophetic precedent for the thousand-year reign of Christ, the Bible frequently talks about the universe-changing events at the end of the Millennium. Without exception, these events are all promised a soon fulfillment:

1. The final judgment was described in all passages and was sworn to occur soon without delay.
2. Jesus promised that Daniel's prophecy about the wicked dead rising at the time of distress would be fulfilled in his generation.
3. Paul and Peter promised the wicked dead would rise soon.
4. Jesus would return at the end of the Millennium and was promised to return soon.
5. Paul promised Christ would crush Satan and death at his approaching return.

Many scholars, including Jewish rabbis living in Jesus' day, did not expect the sixth Millennium, "the days of the Messiah," to last a thousand years. Some even expected it to last forty. Therefore, the honest reader putting himself in the first century Christian mindset, is not bound to take the language literally.

Since the disciples and their generation expected to witness eternity-changing events, the Millennium was approaching its end during their lifetime.

Chapter 9
The Language of Symbols

God often had his prophets write down his messages and prophecies using hyperbole, symbolism, and cosmic imagery. Many times they used a literary technique called "apocalyptic language," which portrayed ancient empire conflicts in dramatic cosmic language.

In order to understand the book of Revelation, one must realize that the author, John, utilized this Old Testament prophet style of writing to convey the dangerous message of the destruction of Jerusalem in the book of Revelation. Cloaking the message with both apocalyptic language and symbolism may very well have been ordained by God in order to get it out safely to warn believers of the soon to come destruction. God "signified," or used signs and symbols, to convey the message of Revelation to John, who wrote it down. This is noted in the very first verse of the book:

> Revelation 1:1 (BLB) The revelation of Jesus Christ, which God gave Him to show to His bond-servants what things it behooves to take place in quickness. And He **signified** it through having sent His angel to His servant, John

When Stars Dissolve

Old Testament prophets Isaiah, Ezekiel, Amos, Joel, and others used spectacular end-of-world cosmic imagery to describe the destruction of a nation, empire, or kingdom (Isaiah 13:10,13; 34:3-5,9-10; Ezekiel 32:7-8; Amos 5:18-22; 8:9; Joel 2:1-5,10). Just one of the many examples of the use of cosmic imagery is found in Isaiah chapter 34, when the prophet wrote about the destruction of Edom.

> Isaiah 34:3-5 (BSB) Their slain will be left unburied, and the stench of their corpses will rise; **the mountains will flow with their blood. 4 All the stars of heaven will be dissolved. The skies will be rolled up like a scroll**, and all their stars will fall like withered leaves from the vine, like foliage from the fig tree. 5 When My sword has drunk its fill in the heavens, then it will come down upon **Edom**, upon the people I have devoted to destruction.

The above language should be understood metaphorically and represents the dramatic experience of a nation being destroyed. Although the "stars of heaven" were not literally "dissolved" when Edom was destroyed and the "skies" were not literally "rolled up like a scroll," from Edom's perspective, it was "lights out."[63] Old Testament prophet Ezekiel wrote in a similar fashion, describing the conquering of Egypt by Babylon.

> Ezekiel 32:1-2,7-8 (WEB) "Yahweh's word came to me, saying, 2 'Son of man, take up a lamentation over **Pharaoh king of Egypt**, and tell him...
>
> 7 **When I extinguish you**, I will cover the heavens **and make its stars dark**. I will cover the sun with a cloud, and the moon won't give its light. 8 **I will make all the bright lights of the sky dark over you, and set darkness on your land**," says the Lord Yahweh.

---

[63] Rosenauer, Joel. 2023. "Proceed With Caution." YouTube. https://www.youtube.com/watch?v=FFpzKVWvAVw.

Another example of apocalyptic language can be found when Isaiah describes the complete destruction of Babylon by the Medes.

> Isaiah 13:1,10,13,17 (ESV) **The oracle concerning Babylon**...
>
> 10 For the **stars of the heavens and their constellations will not give their light**; the sun will be dark at its rising, and the moon will not shed its light...
>
> 13 Therefore I will make **the heavens tremble, and the earth will be shaken out of its place**, at the wrath of the LORD of hosts in the day of his fierce anger...
>
> 17 Behold, I am stirring up the Medes against them...

In like manner, John, who was familiar with the writings of the prophets, signified the message using apocalyptic end-of-the-world cosmic imagery to describe the destruction of Jerusalem in the book of Revelation.

> Revelation 6:13-14 (NASB 1995) **and the stars of the sky fell to the earth**, as a fig tree casts its unripe figs when shaken by a great wind. **The sky was split apart like a scroll** when it is rolled up, and **every mountain and island were moved out of their places.**

Revelation was written using the same literary style as the Old Testament prophets and must be interpreted accordingly.

The Symbols of Revelation

In keeping with Revelation's literary style, the beasts, witnesses, and a prostitute contained in its pages symbolized *beastly* or *unfaithful* kingdoms, individuals, and themes with which first century Christians would have been familiar.

In the vision, the angel told John to interpret the seven heads of the sea beast as "seven kings" and "seven hills." This is a clear indication that "the beast" was a symbol for evil kings and kingdoms and not a literal creature.

> Revelation 17:9-10 (ESV) This calls for a mind with wisdom: **the seven heads** [of the sea beast] **are seven mountains** on which the woman is seated; 10 **they are also seven kings**, five of whom have fallen, one is, the other has not yet come, and when he does come he must remain only a little while.

Identifying the Characters

Revelation was written to first century Christians concerning events that were about to take place. The reader must put themselves into the shoes of Revelation's audience to interpret the symbols from their perspective. Fortunately, the events and characters of the first century were so spectacular that it is hard to deny they were the fulfillment of Revelation's prophecies. However, there are different theories as to the exact interpretation of the symbols involved in this period of history.

Avid Bible researchers actively debate the identities of the symbols of Revelation, bringing evidence to support their views. Discussions on this topic continue through end times blogs, Facebook groups, and books with different interpretations of the symbology. The land beast is one hotly debated topic (see "Chapter 13 The Land Beast"). While Daniel Morais believes that the identity of both the land and sea beast are connected to first century Rome, Kurt M. Simmons[64] and David Chilton[65] make a strong case that the land beast was a first century Jewish entity. Adam Maarschalk argues both the land and sea beast were Jewish entities.[66] While alternate theories may prove true and bring a satisfying explanation to Revelation's mysteries, the most compelling and comprehensive view is based on Daniel Morais' work and will be presented here.

The Bible helps the reader interpret symbols by giving many clues about the characters; in fact, sometimes it even identifies them. The dragon is the best example of this:

> Revelation 12:9 (ESV) And the great dragon was thrown down, that ancient serpent, **who is called the devil and Satan**, the deceiver of the whole world—he was thrown down to the earth, and his angels were thrown down with him.

John clearly identified the dragon as Satan. With the Bible helping to interpret these symbols, the following chapters will identify the characters below:

---

[64] Simmons, Kurt M. 2010. Revelation Explained: A Contemporary Historical Analysis of the Apocalypse. N.p.: Biblical Publishing.

[65] Chilton, David. 1987. The Days of Vengeance: An Exposition of the Book of Revelation. N.p.: Dominion Press. https://www.reconstructionistradio.com/audiobook/the-days-of-vengeance/chapter-3-leviathan-and-behemoth-9/.

[66] Maarschalk, Adam. n.d. "Beast of Revelation – Pursuing Truth." Adam Maarschalk. Accessed December 31, 2022. https://adammaarschalk.com/beast-of-revelation/.

1. The prostitute was the great city where the Lord was crucified, or Jerusalem (Revelation 11:8; 17:18).
2. The sea beast was an archetype of the general conquerors of God's people whom saints should avoid (Revelation 17:8). In the first century, Rome and its Caesars were the seven heads (Revelation 17:9-10).
    a. The eighth king of the sea beast was Vespasian and Titus, who later jointly became the eighth Caesars (Revelation 17:11).
    b. The two witnesses likely represented the spirits or manner of two prominent prophets sharing the body of Jesus ben Ananus (Revelation 11:8 [LSV]).
    c. Apollyon, leader of the locust armies, was represented by the eighth Caesar Titus (Revelation 9:1-2; 11:7; 17:8; 17:11).
3. The ten horns of the sea beast (Revelation 13:1) were ten Jewish generals (Revelation 17:12).
4. The two horns of the land beast were Vespasian and Titus, who both resurrected out of the severed head of the sea beast, or Nero (Revelation 13:11). Vespasian was also the False Prophet (Revelation 16:13; 19:20; 20:10) and false Messiah, the lamb that spoke like a dragon (Revelation 13:11).

The following research is based primarily on some of the thorough and intriguing work of Daniel Morais at https://

revelationrevolution.org and contributions from other perceptive researchers.

Chapter 10
Jerusalem, the Prostitute

The most important character to identify in Revelation is the prostitute. The prostitute was the "great city," apostate Jerusalem of the first century. More specifically, the prostitute was the unbelieving Jews that crucified Jesus and were loyal to Rome.

> Revelation 17:18 (ESV) And **the woman that you saw is the great city** that has dominion over the kings of the earth.

The angel earlier identified the "great city" as the place where Jesus was crucified. This could only be one city, first century Jerusalem.

> Revelation 11:8 (ESV) and their dead bodies will lie in the street of **the great city** that symbolically is called Sodom and Egypt, **where their Lord was crucified**.

The great city was symbolically called "Sodom and Egypt" (Revelation 11:8). The Song of Moses prophesied that Israel would be like Sodom in the last days (Deuteronomy 32:15,20-21,29,32). Paul confirmed that the Song of Moses concerned first-century Israel (Romans 10:19).

Why was Jerusalem a prostitute? Because she was having an adulterous affair with Rome. She crucified Jesus, her true king, and declared Caesar her ruler (John 19:15-16).

> John 19:15-16 (ESV) They cried out, "Away with him, away with him, crucify him!" Pilate said to them, "Shall I crucify your King?" **The chief priests answered, "We have no king**

but Caesar." 16 So he delivered him over to them to be crucified.

Revelation 17:1-5 (ESV) Then one of the seven angels who had the seven bowls came and said to me, "Come, I will show you the **judgment of the great prostitute who is seated on many waters, 2 with whom the kings of the earth have committed sexual immorality,** and with the wine of whose sexual immorality the dwellers on earth have become drunk." 3 And he carried me away in the Spirit into a wilderness, and I saw a woman sitting on a scarlet beast that was full of blasphemous names, and it had seven heads and ten horns. 4 The woman was arrayed in purple and scarlet, and adorned with gold and jewels and pearls, holding in her hand a golden **cup full of abominations and the impurities of her sexual immorality. 5 And on her forehead was written a name of mystery: "Babylon the great, mother of prostitutes and of earth's abominations."**

The prostitute was drunk with the blood of the martyrs and saints.

Revelation 17:6 (ESV) And I saw the woman, drunk with the blood of the saints, the blood of the martyrs of Jesus.

Jesus told the Pharisees that they would be held responsible for all the blood of the martyrs and saints, when he said to them:

Matthew 23:34-37 (ESV) Therefore I send you prophets and wise men and scribes, some of **whom you will kill and crucify**, and some you will flog in your synagogues and persecute from town to town, 35 so that **on you may come all the righteous blood shed on earth**, from the blood of righteous Abel to the blood of Zechariah the son of

> Barachiah, whom you murdered between the sanctuary and the altar. 36 Truly, I say to you, all these things will come upon this generation.
>
> 37 "**O Jerusalem, Jerusalem, the city that kills the prophets and stones those who are sent to it!** How often would I have gathered your children together as a hen gathers her brood under her wings, and you were not willing! 38 See, your house is left to you desolate.
>
> *See also Luke 11:46-51.*

In the Old Covenant, Babylon, Sodom, and Egypt were enemies of God's people and persecuted Israel. In the first century, unbelieving Jerusalem acted as an enemy to New Covenant Israel when they crucified Christ (Acts 4:10) and persecuted believers (Matthew 10:17-23; Luke 11:46-51; Romans 9:27; Galatians 4:29; 1 Thessalonians 2:14-16; Revelation 2:9; 3:9).

> 1 Thessalonians 2:14-16 (ESV) For you, brothers, became imitators of the churches of God in Christ Jesus that are in Judea. For you suffered the same things from your own countrymen as they did from the Jews, 15 who killed both the Lord Jesus and the prophets, and drove us out, and displease God and oppose all mankind 16 by hindering us from speaking to the Gentiles that they might be saved—so as always to fill up the measure of their sins.

Hence, Revelation refers to unbelieving Jerusalem as Babylon, Sodom, and Egypt (Matthew 23:30-38; Revelation 11:8; 18:21,24). In Revelation, ethnic but faithless Jews were never defined as God's people. That title was reserved for those who had faith in Christ. The verse below shows that in Revelation the "saints" are those who "keep the commandments of God and their faith in Jesus."

> Revelation 14:12 (ESV) Here is a call for the endurance of the saints, those who keep the commandments of God and their faith in Jesus.

Throughout the Old Covenant, God chose to work almost exclusively with ethnic Jews, to be their God (Amos 3:2). When he established the New Covenant, the Gentiles were invited into God's people, "Israel." Those who rejected Christ were removed from being God's people, even if they were ethnic Jews (Matthew 3:9; 8:5-11; 21:43; 22:1-10; 24:14; Acts 3:21-26; Romans 4:11-12; 9:6-8,27; 11:17-18; Galatians 3:29; 4:21-31; Ephesians 2:11-22; Colossians 1:26-27).

> Romans 11:17-18 (ESV) But if some of the branches were broken off [unbelieving Jews], and you [Gentiles], although a wild olive shoot, were grafted in among the others and now share in the nourishing root of the olive tree, 18 do not be arrogant toward the branches. If you are, remember it is not you who support the root, but the root that supports you.

Like the wild olive tree, those Jews who rejected the faith and Christ as their Messiah were broken off from God's people Israel, and the Gentiles who came to the faith were grafted into the tree. To be Abraham's descendant and part of God's people, one must be his child through faith, not blood.

> Romans 9:6-8 (ESV) But it is not as though the word of God has failed. **For not all who are descended from Israel belong to Israel**, 7 and not all are children of Abraham

> because they are his offspring, but "Through Isaac shall your offspring be named." 8 This means that it is not the children of the flesh who are the children of God, but the children of the promise are counted as offspring.
>
> Matthew 3:9 (ESV) And do not presume to say to yourselves, 'We have Abraham as our father,' for I tell you, God is able from these stones to raise up children for Abraham.
>
> Galatians 3:29 (ESV) And if you are Christ's, then you are Abraham's offspring, heirs according to promise.

Just like Ishmael was cast out from Abraham's people when he persecuted Isaac, the unbelieving Jews were cast out of the kingdom, and only the children of promise were considered the true children of Abraham.

> Matthew 21:43 (ESV) Therefore I tell you, the kingdom of God will be taken away from you [chief priests and the elders of the people] and given to a people producing its fruits.

Paul compares Hagar and Sarah to the two covenants. The Old Covenant (Hagar) bears children by physical descent while the New Covenant (Sarah) bears children by faith.

> Galatians 4:21-31 (ESV) Tell me, you who desire to be under the law, do you not listen to the law? For it is written that Abraham had two sons, one by a slave woman and one by a free woman. But the son of the slave was born according to the flesh, while the son of the free woman was born through promise. Now this may be interpreted allegorically: **these women are two covenants**. One is from Mount Sinai, bearing children for slavery; she is Hagar. **Now Hagar is Mount Sinai in Arabia; she corresponds to**

> **the present [first century] Jerusalem, for she is in slavery with her children.** But the Jerusalem above is free, and she is our mother. For it is written,
>
> "Rejoice, O barren one who does not bear;
>
> break forth and cry aloud, you who are not in labor!
>
> For the children of the desolate one will be more
>
> than those of the one who has a husband."
>
> Now you, brothers, like Isaac, are children of promise. But just as at that time he who was born according to the flesh persecuted him who was born according to the Spirit, so also it is now. But what does the Scripture say? **"Cast out the slave woman and her son, for the son of the slave woman shall not inherit with the son of the free woman."** So, brothers, we are not children of the slave but of the free woman.

As shown, God cast out the unbelieving Jews of the Old Covenant.

Today, Jews and Gentiles are invited into the kingdom through faith in Jesus Christ; God shows no favoritism to one group or the other (Galatians 3:28).

Now that the prostitute is identified as apostate Jerusalem, on what beast did she ride?

Roman standard bearers which headed each Roman legion wore skins of lions, leopards, and bears.[68]

The Seven Heads

> Revelation 13:1 (ESV) And I saw a beast rising out of the sea, with ten horns and seven heads, with ten diadems on its horns and blasphemous names on its heads.

The symbolism of the seven heads of the Leviathan in Revelation 13:1 are explained further in Revelation 17. There, the angel tells John the seven heads are seven kings and seven hills.

> Revelation 17:9-10 (ESV) This calls for a mind with wisdom: the seven heads are seven mountains on which the woman is seated; 10 they are also seven kings, five of whom have fallen, one is, the other has not yet come, and when he does come he must remain only a little while.

Rome was a city built on seven hills.[69] From the birth of Christ through the civil war of Rome, Rome had seven Caesars:

1. Julius
2. Augustus
3. Tiberius
4. Gaius

---

[68] Morais, Daniel. n.d. "Revelation 13: A Preterist Commentary." Revelation Revolution Foundation. Accessed December 10, 2022. https://www.revelationrevolution.org/revelation-13-a-preterist-commentary/.

[69] "Seven hills of Rome." n.d. Wikipedia. Accessed December 10, 2022. https://en.wikipedia.org/wiki/Seven_hills_of_Rome.

5. Claudius
6. Nero
7. Galba

The Romans considered the reigns of Otho and Vitellius to be illegitimate and a rebellion.[70] The joint reign of Titus and Vespasian as the eighth king will be explained later.

It was said that when the seventh king came he would "remain only a little while" (Revelation 17:10 [ESV]). Galba, the seventh Roman Emperor, only reigned for seven months before being killed.

The Head Was Wounded

> Revelation 13:3 (ESV) One of its heads seemed to have a mortal wound, but its mortal wound was healed, and the whole earth marveled as they followed the beast.

---

[70] Otho's emperorship was considered illegitimate and a rebellion by the Romans and was only confirmed by the Senate through the threat of force. He later surrendered his reign to Vitellius, who likewise was seen as illegitimate. "Otho withdrew from the battle, declaring that he could not witness a battle between kindred — just as if he had become emperor in some legitimate fashion and had not murdered the consuls, the Caesar, and the emperor in Rome itself"; "Thus, after living most disgracefully of all men, he died most nobly; and though he had seized the empire by a most villainous deed, his taking leave of it was most honorable."; "At the same time that this happened, Vespasian, who was engaged in warfare with the Jews, learned of the rebellion of Vitellius and Otho and was deliberating what he should do." (Dio, Cassius. 1914. Roman History. Translated by Earnest Cary. Loeb Classical Library ed. 9 vols. N.p.: Harvard University Press. https://penelope.uchicago.edu/Thayer/E/Roman/Texts/Cassius_Dio/64*.html, 64.65.8; 64.10; 64.15; 65.8).

Symbols in Revelation sometimes represent more than one thing. For example, the seven heads of the beast were said to be both seven kings *and* seven hills (Revelation 17:9-10).

On June 9, 68 AD, Nero, the sixth Caesar, stabbed himself in the throat with a dagger, fulfilling the prophecy that one head of the beast "was wounded by the sword" (Revelation 13:14).[71] Moreover, the kingdom of the beast was also wounded.

> Revelation 16:10 (ESV) The fifth angel poured out his bowl on the throne of the beast, **and its kingdom was plunged into darkness.**

Nero's death caused a long and dreadful civil war in Rome that most expected would result in its downfall.[72]

A *mortal* wound is one that results in death (Revelation 13:3,12). Nero's wound had resulted in his and the Roman empire's death; hence, the empire was cast into darkness.

To all appearances, the symbology of Revelation 13:3 intends a double fulfillment.

---

[71] Tranquillus, Caius S. 1914. The Life of Nero, The Lives of the Twelve Caesars. Translated by John C. Rolfe. N.p.: Loeb Classical Library edition. http://penelope.uchicago.edu/Thayer/E/Roman/Texts/Suetonius/12Caesars/Nero*.html, 49.3.

[72] 4 Ezra 12:18; Tacitus, The History, 1.11, http://www.perseus.tufts.edu/hopper/text?doc=Tac.+Hist.+1.11&fromdoc=Perseus%3Atext%3A1999.02.0080; Josephus, War, 4.10.2, 4.11.5.

The Wound Was Healed

> Revelation 13:3 (ESV) One of its heads seemed to have a mortal wound, **but its mortal wound was healed**, and the whole earth marveled as they followed the beast.

Both the head of the beast and its kingdom were resurrected from the dead. As more evidence, in two places in Revelation, the sea beast is said to return from the "bottomless pit." Coming out of the bottomless pit is a picture of a resurrection from Sheol, which is sometimes described in the Bible as a "pit" (Psalm 30:3).

> Revelation 17:8 (ESV) The beast that you saw was, and is not, **and is about to rise from the bottomless pit** and go to destruction.

> Revelation 11:7 (ESV) And when they have finished their testimony, **the beast that rises from the bottomless pit** will make war on them and conquer them and kill them

The above prophecies should be understood to mean that the severed head and kingdom of the beast would be resurrected.

In the legend of Hercules, when one head of the Hydra or Leviathan was cut off, two grew in its place.[73] The Roman civil war ended when Nero was replaced by Vespasian and Titus, who came to power as joint Caesars on December 22, 69 AD

---

[73] Apollodorus. 1921. Apollodorus, The Library. Translated by James G. Frazer. Loeb Classical Library ed. 2 vols. Cambridge, MA: Harvard University Press. http://www.perseus.tufts.edu/hopper/text?doc=Perseus:text:1999.01.0022:text=Library, 2.5.2, http://www.perseus.tufts.edu/hopper/text?doc=Perseus%3Atext%3A1999.01.0022%3Atext%3DLibrary%3Abook%3D2%3Achapter%3D5%3Asection%3D2.

(Kislev 18) and brought order back to the empire.[74] Additionally, rumors spread that Nero was seen alive and well a year after his death.[75]

The Leviathan Demanded Worship

> Revelation 13:4 (ESV) And they worshiped the dragon, for he had given his authority to the beast

The Romans forced their inhabitants to honor their gods and idols. This is how they led the world to worship the dragon (Satan).

Additionally, some Caesars demanded to be worshiped as gods, even calling themselves "almighty god," "king of kings," and "lord of lords." In the same way, the beast "utters proud words and blasphemies" (Revelation 13:5) and "was full of blasphemous names" (Revelation 17:3). Titus insulted the God of Israel, committed blasphemies in the temple, and claimed to have slain God.[76]

The Leviathan Was Undefeatable

> Revelation 13:4,7 (ESV) ...and they worshiped the beast, saying, "Who is like the beast, and who can fight against

---

74 McKenzie, Duncan W. 2009. The Antichrist and the Second Coming: A Preterist Examination. Vol. II. N.p.: Xulon Press, Incorporated, 191.

75 Tacitus, The History, 2.8, http://www.perseus.tufts.edu/hopper/text?doc=Perseus%3Atext%3A1999.02.0080%3Abook%3D2%3Achapter%3D8; Suetonius, Nero, 57.2, http://penelope.uchicago.edu/Thayer/E/Roman/Texts/Suetonius/12Caesars/Nero*.html.

76 "Babylonian Talmud: Tractate Gittin." n.d. Chabad.org. Accessed December 10, 2022. https://www.chabad.org/media/pdf/323/YIxQ3233957.pdf, 56b.

> it?" ...7 authority was given it over every tribe and people and language and nation

In an inspiring and dreadful speech, Roman king Agrippa attempted to persuade the Jews to avoid war with Rome, illustrating how the Roman Empire decimated all empires that stood against it.[77] No one could wage war against Rome (Revelation 13:4). It had authority over every tribe and nation of the earth (Revelation 13:7).

As the scripture pointed out, who could fight against it?

Conquered for Forty-Two Months

> Revelation 13:5,7 (ESV) ...and it was allowed to exercise authority for forty-two months... 7 Also it was allowed to make war on the saints and to conquer them.

Although the exact date of Vespasian and Titus' arrival in Judea is unknown, it is estimated that Vespasian and Titus arrived in Jerusalem in early March of 67 AD. Their crusade against Judea continued for forty-two months, ending on September 2, 70 AD (Elul 8). Nero also hunted down and tortured Christians across the Roman empire for forty-two months, from mid-November 64 AD to June 9, 68 AD (Mar Cheshvan - Sivan 19) after blaming

[77] Josephus, War, 2.16.

them for a fire that broke out in Rome.[78] Concerning this persecution, Church historian J. L. von Mosheim wrote,

> "Foremost in the rank of those emperors, on whom the church looks back with horror as her persecutors, stands Nero, a prince whose conduct towards the Christians admits of no palliation, but was to the last degree unprincipled and inhuman. The dreadful persecution which took place by order of this tyrant, commenced at Rome about the middle of November, in the year of our Lord 64. . . . This dreadful persecution ceased but with the death of Nero. The empire, it is well known, was not delivered from the tyranny of this monster until the year 68, when he put an end to his own life."[79]

In both these ways, the beast exercised authority for forty-two months (Revelation 13:5) and was allowed to make war on the saints (Revelation 13:7). Jesus said, "as you did it to one of the least of these my brothers, you did it to me" (Matthew 25:40 [ESV]). Hence, when the Romans attacked Christians, they were attacking Christ, fulfilling the prophecy that their armies

---

[78] Schaff, Philip. 1996. History of the Christian church. N.p.: Hendrickson Publishers. https://ccel.org/ccel/schaff/hcc1/hcc1.i.VI.37.html; Stevens, Edward E., and Michael A. Nichols. 2014. Final Decade Before the End: Jewish and Christian History Just Before the Jewish Revolt. Bradford, Pennsylvania: International Preterist Association, 155-157; Tertullian. 1885. Apology, From Ante-Nicene Fathers. Edited by Alexander Roberts, James Donaldson, A. C. Coxe., and Kevin Knight. Translated by S. Thelwall. Vol. 3. Buffalo, NY: Christian Literature Publishing Co. https://www.newadvent.org/fathers/0301.htm, 1.5 (3.22).

[79] Von Mosheim, Johann L. 2006. Historical Commentaries on the State of Christianity During the First Three Hundred and Twenty-Five Years from the Christian Era, 2 Volumes. Edited by James Murdock. Translated by Robert S. Vidal. (As cited in http://www.ecclesia.org/truth/beast.html) ed. N.p.: Wipf & Stock Publishers.

"make war against him who was sitting on the horse" (Revelation 19:19 [ESV]).

When the Roman armies first arrived, Christians who heeded Jesus' warning in the Olivet Discourse fled to the town of Pella in the mountains, thereby escaping a portion of these tribulations: their tribulation was "cut short" (Matthew 24:22 [ESV]). Those who did not flee[80] when angelic armies were seen on the clouds, suffered the wrath of the Romans during the invasion of Jerusalem (Matthew 24:17-22; Revelation 6:9-11; 7:9-14; 12:13-17; 13:7).[81]

Was, and Is Not

How is it that the Leviathan "now is not" in Revelation 17:8 and yet "is" in Revelation 17:10 at the time of John's writing?

> Revelation 17:8 (ESV) The beast that you saw was, and **is not**, and is about to rise from the bottomless pit and go to destruction.
>
> Revelation 17:9 (ESV) This calls for a mind with wisdom: the seven heads are seven mountains on which the woman is seated; 10 they are also seven kings, five of whom have fallen, **one is**, the other has not yet come, and when he does come he must remain only a little while.

[80] Maarschalk, 2017.

[81] Severus, Sulpitius. 1894. Sacred History, Nicene and Post-Nicene Fathers, Second Series. Edited by Philip Schaff, Henry Wace, and Kevin Knight. Translated by Alexander Roberts. Vol. 11. 14 vols. Buffalo, NY: Christian Literature Publishing Co. https://www.newadvent.org/fathers/3505.htm, 2.30.7, https://www.newadvent.org/fathers/35052.htm.

When Revelation says "one is" (Revelation 17:10), it refers to the sixth Caesar, meaning that Nero was reigning at the time Revelation was written. (Revelation was written between 62-64 AD, according to Ed Stevens.[82])

Therefore, one must interpret "is not" specifically to mean the eighth king, or eighth Caesar.

> Revelation 17:11 (BLB) And **the beast which was, and is not, is also himself an eighth**, and is of the seven, and goes into destruction.

The word "also," included in the Greek, should be noted. The Leviathan was not exclusively the eighth king, but was "also" the eighth king. The Leviathan, and more specifically the eighth king, was not merely an end time tyrant or kingdom, but an archetype of the enemies of God's people in past conflicts. Egypt/Pharaoh (Ezekiel 29:2-3) and Babylon/Nebuchadnezzar (Jeremiah 51:34) were described as "serpents" or "beasts" towards Israel, and those prophets who held to the testimony of the Messiah suffered at their hands. Likewise, nearly two hundred years prior to the writing of Revelation, Antiochus Epiphanes desecrated the Jewish temple, and thus he also followed the archetype of the beast.

The eighth king would follow in the footsteps of the Leviathan in its previous forms but was not yet in power at the time of John's writing (Revelation 17:11). Who was the eighth king?

---

[82] Stevens, The Final Decade, 84.

The Eighth King

During the Roman civil war following Nero's death, Galba ascended to the throne and was confirmed by the Senate. However, Galba was killed after seven months by a rebellion led by Otho and later Vitellius. The Romans considered the reigns of Otho and Vitellius to be illegitimate and characterized them as rebellions. Vespasian became the eighth legitimate Emperor and jointly reigned with his son Titus. Like Antiochus Epiphanes, Titus desecrated the temple. Just as John the Baptist was the archetype of Elijah, Titus was the archetype of Antiochus Epiphanes.

The Two Witnesses

The eighth king was the beast who rose from the bottomless pit (Revelation 17:8,11). The beast who rose from the bottomless pit in Revelation 11:7-8 was expected to kill the two witnesses in the streets of the "great city" or Jerusalem.

> Revelation 11:7-8 (ESV) And when they have finished their testimony, the beast that rises from the bottomless pit will make war on them and conquer them and kill them, 8 and their dead bodies will lie in the street of the great city that symbolically is called Sodom and Egypt, where their Lord was crucified.

The two witnesses seemed to point to Jesus ben Ananus, whom Titus killed with a Roman stone catapulted at the beginning of the siege of Jerusalem.[83] Although Revelation said there were

---

[83] Josephus, War, 6.5.3.

two witnesses, it mentions them sharing one body. The Greek literally reads, "and **their body [is]** on the street of the great city that is called spiritually Sodom and Egypt, where also their Lord was crucified" (Revelation 11:8 [LSV]).[84] In a couple places in the Bible, men operated in the spirit or manner of a prominent prophet. John the Baptist came in the spirit of Elijah (Matthew 17:9-13; Luke 1:16–17). Elisha received a "double portion" of Elijah's spirit (2 Kings 2:9). Perhaps the spirits of two prominent prophets shared the body of Jesus ben Ananus.

(Morais argues Jesus ben Ananus was Jesus Christ himself.[85])

Apollyon and the Locust Armies

There appears to be a connection between the eighth king of the sea beast and Apollyon, the king of the locust armies (Revelation 9:11). Both the eighth king and Apollyon came out of the bottomless pit (Revelation 9:1-2; 11:7; 17:8).

Apollyon led the locust armies out of the abyss to torment those without God's seal for five months (Revelation 9). The Roman god Apollo considered locusts sacred creatures. Occasionally in the Bible humans were called angels (2 Chronicles 36:15-16; Haggai 1:13; Malachi 3:1; Matthew 11:10;

---

84 "Revelation 11:8 Greek Text Analysis." n.d. Bible Hub. Accessed December 26, 2022. https://biblehub.com/text/revelation/11-8.htm.

85 Morais, Daniel. n.d. "Revelation 11: A Preterist Commentary–Who are the Two Witnesses?" Revelation Revolution Foundation. Accessed December 10, 2022. https://www.revelationrevolution.org/revelation-11-a-preterist-commentary-who-are-the-two-witnesses/.

24:31; Luke 7:24; 9:52; 1 Timothy 3:16; Revelation 2:1,8,12,18; 3:1,7,14; 21:17). Titus was the leader of "Legio XV Apollinaris" ("Apollo's Fifteenth Legion"), and besieged Jerusalem for five months before destroying it. Morais lays out far more fascinating correlations and lines of evidence of this interpretation.[86]

Thrown Into the Lake of Fire

The sea beast was thrown into the lake of fire.

> Revelation 19:20 (ESV) And the beast was captured, and with it the false prophet [see Chapter 13 The Land Beast] who in its presence had done the signs by which he deceived those who had received the mark of the beast and those who worshiped its image. These two were thrown alive into the lake of fire that burns with sulfur.

In the above passage, the beast was "thrown *alive* into the lake of fire." The lake of fire was a picture of the afterlife punishment that awaited the enemies of Christ. Recall that Satan was also cast into the lake of fire (Revelation 20:10).

The sense in which Rome was "thrown alive" into the lake of fire occurred in 79 AD when Mount Vesuvius erupted and instantly destroyed two entire coastline cities of Rome while

---

[86] Morais, Revelation 9, https://www.revelationrevolution.org/revelation-9-a-preterist-commentary-who-is-apollyon/.

the populace was inside.[87] Indeed, the instantaneous death caused by a searing pyroclastic surge wave left petrified human cavities in the ash, preserving their form and expressions to this day.[88] Interestingly, Satan was also "thrown into the lake of fire" a year after the volcano eruption when a fire destroyed most or all the Satanic temples in Rome.[89]

Summary

Rome and its seven Caesars met all of the requirements of the Leviathan and its seven heads (Revelation 13:1-8).

- Rome resembled a leopard, bear, and lion (Revelation 13:2) because it had conquered much of the land of Greece, Media/Persia, and Babylon and included their religions in its culture.
- The heads of the beast were the seven Caesars of Rome, Julius through Galba, who reigned from the time of the birth of Christ through the siege in Jerusalem. (Revelation 17:9-10).

---

[87] Dio, Cassius. 1914. Roman History. Translated by Earnest Cary. Loeb Classical Library ed. 9 vols. N.p.: Harvard University Press. https://penelope.uchicago.edu/Thayer/E/Roman/Texts/Cassius_Dio/home.html, 66.23.3, https://penelope.uchicago.edu/Thayer/e/roman/texts/cassius_dio/66*.html.

[88] Dimuro, Gina. 2018. "39 Agonizing Photos Of Pompeii's Bodies Frozen In Time." All That's Interesting. https://allthatsinteresting.com/bodies-of-pompeii.

[89] Dio, Roman History, 66.24, https://penelope.uchicago.edu/Thayer/e/roman/texts/cassius_dio/66*.html.

- The sea beast and its kingdom were wounded and thrown into darkness when Nero, the sixth Caesar, stabbed himself in the neck and caused a long and dreadful civil war in Rome (Revelation 13:3; 16:10).
- The sea beast recovered from its wound under the joint reign of "heads," Caesars Vespasian and Titus, who took the throne and brought back order to Rome (Revelation 11:7; 13:3; 17:8).
- Just as the sea beast made the world worship Satan and had seven heads with blasphemous names, the Romans demanded the world honor their gods and worship the Caesars as gods (Revelation 13:5; 17:3-4).
- Rome was undefeatable and conquered any nation that stood against it; people worshiped its might (Revelation 13:4,7).
- Rome attacked Jerusalem for forty-two months, and Nero persecuted Christians for forty-two months; thereby the beast exercised authority for forty-two months and made war on the saints (Revelation 13:5,7).
- The beast "was, and is not" (Revelation 17:8) because it was not only Rome and its Caesars but an archetype of the enemies of God's people who persecuted the saints in the past. Pharoah and Nebuchadnezzar were also called beasts in the Old Testament (Ezekiel 29:2-3; Jeremiah 51:34).

- The sea beast was also an eighth king (Revelation 17:11), or Vespasian and Titus, who besieged Jerusalem.
- After the sea beast came out of the abyss, it killed the two witnesses in Jerusalem (Revelation 11:7-8). Titus likewise killed the prophet Jesus ben Ananus at the beginning of the siege of Jerusalem.
- Titus led "Apollo's Fifteenth Legion" to torment the residents of Jerusalem for five months in the same way Apollyon led the locust armies to siege those with the mark of the beast for five months (Revelation 9:1-11).
- Rome was thrown *alive* into a lake of fire, when Mount Vesuvius erupted in 79 AD, instantly destroying two coastline cities near Rome (Revelation 19:20).

Rome and its seven Caesars fulfilled each prophecy concerning the sea beast. However, the beast also had ten horns (Revelation 13:1). The sea beast was not exclusively Rome and its Caesars, but was also the Jewish zealots (the ten kings/ten horns) who worked with Rome to attack Christianity.

Chapter 12
The Ten Horns

The sea beast had ten horns (Revelation 13:1) and fortunately, the angel helped identify these horns.

> Revelation 17:12-14 (ESV) And the ten horns that you saw are ten **kings who have not yet received royal power**, but they are to receive authority as kings for one hour, together with the beast. 13 These are of one mind, and they hand over their power and authority to the beast. 14 They will make war on the Lamb, and the Lamb will conquer them, for he is Lord of lords and King of kings, and those with him are called and chosen and faithful."

The ten horns of the Leviathan were ten kings who had yet to receive power. Hence, they could not include Nero or other entities that existed during the writing of Revelation. However, some time after Revelation was written, in late November 66 AD, after Roman general Cestius Gallus failed to conquer Jerusalem, the Jewish zealots elected ten generals from among the Jews to help fight Rome.[90]

1. Joseph, the son of Gorion
2. Ananus, the high priest
3. Jesus, the son of Sapphias
4. Eleazar, the son of Ananias
5. Niger, the then-governor of Idumea

---

[90]Josephus, War, 2.20.3-4.

6. Joseph, the son of Simon
7. Manasseh
8. John, the Esscue
9. John, the son of Matthias
10. Josephus, the son of Matthias (the same Josephus who later became a historian and wrote "The War of the Jews")

The above ten generals fulfilled all the prophecies of the ten horns of the sea beast. The symbology of the above Bible passage will be explained in detail in the following sections.

Surrender Their Power to the Beast

When Titus arrived for the final siege of Jerusalem, only three of the ten Jewish generals could fight against him.

> Daniel 7:24 (ESV) As for the ten horns, out of this kingdom ten kings shall arise, and another shall arise after them; he shall be different from the former ones, and shall put down **three kings**.

These three "surrendered" to Rome (a more accurate translation according to Stephen S. Smalley[91]) and fulfilled the prophecy that they "hand over their power and authority to the beast."

> Revelation 17:13 (ESV) These are of one mind, and they hand over their power and authority to the beast.

---

[91]Smalley, Stephen S. 2012. The Revelation to John: A Commentary on the Greek Text of the Apocalypse. N.p.: InterVarsity Press.

Power for an Hour

John said the ten horns obtained “authority as kings for one hour” (Revelation 17:12 [ESV]).

> Revelation 17:12 (ESV) And the ten horns that you saw... **are to receive authority as kings for one hour**...

The ten Jewish generals reigned from late 66 AD to mid 70 AD before they were entirely defeated, lasting a short period of less than three and a half years.

A Roman and Jewish Leviathan

“How could these ten horns be Jewish if the beast was Roman?” As discussed, symbols in Revelation sometimes represent more than one thing. Just as the angel said the seven heads were seven hills, both Jerusalem and Rome were cities built on seven hills.[92] Recall that in Revelation 17:3, the prostitute (apostate Jerusalem) was seated on the sea beast (Rome). The Romans and the ten Jewish generals played primary antagonists in helping to destroy Jerusalem.

During the war with Rome, the Jews were divided between those loyal to Rome and those wanting freedom from it.[93] These two factions betrayed, killed, and hated each other.[94] The seditious Jews hated their brethrens’ loyalty to Rome and

---

[92] "List of cities claimed to be built on seven hills." n.d. Wikipedia. Accessed December 10, 2022. https://en.wikipedia.org/wiki/List_of_cities_claimed_to_be_built_on_seven_hills.

[93] Josephus, War, 3.9.7-8, 3.10.4, 4.3.2-3.

[94] Josephus, War, 4.3.9-12.

helped to bring about the destruction of Jerusalem through their robberies, barbarity, and their provocations of Rome. Describing these seditious Jews, Josephus said, "Although these very men, besides the seditions they raised, were otherwise the direct cause of the city's destruction also."[95] Thus, the ten horns, or ten Jewish generals, hated the prostitute and made her desolate.

> Revelation 17:16 (ESV) And the ten horns that you saw, they and the beast will hate the prostitute. They will make her desolate and naked, and devour her flesh and burn her up with fire

Since Revelation is primarily concerned about Christianity, not unbelieving Israel, the beast represented the zealots and Roman partnership against Christianity.

The Ten Kings: Enemies of Christ

Ananus, the high priest and one of the ten Jewish generals, killed Jesus' brother James and expelled the Christians from Jerusalem in 62 AD[96] before becoming a general.

The Jewish zealots also mocked God by flagrantly breaking his law, breaking their oaths, and committing atrocities during the

---

[95] Josephus, War, 4.3.3.

[96] "Alexandria, Eutychius o. 2014. The Annals. Translated by Roger Pearse. https://www.roger-pearse.com/weblog/eutychius-annals-my-posts-containing-the-translation/, 9.7, https://www.roger-pearse.com/weblog/2015/01/10/the-annals-of-eutychius-of-alexandria-10th-c-ad-chapter-9-contd/.

Sabbath.[97] In this way, the ten horns of the beast made war against the Rider (Revelation 19:19).

> Revelation 19:19 (ESV) And I saw the beast and the kings of the earth with their armies gathered to make war against him who was sitting on the horse and against his army.

The Ten Kings Were Destroyed

The beast was captured and thrown into the lake of fire (Revelation 19:20). Although Rome was thrown alive into the lake of fire at the eruption of Mount Vesuvius, the ten horns of the beast, or the ten Jewish generals, were thrown alive into the lake of fire during the siege of Jerusalem. Most generals had fallen by the final siege, but those who remained were killed in Jerusalem's flames or afterward when they were captured and put to death in Rome.

Summary

The ten Jewish generals, or ten kings, fulfilled all the prophecies concerning the ten horns of the sea beast.

- The ten Jewish generals, like the ten horns of the sea beast, did not have power when Revelation was written (between 62-64 AD, according to Ed Stevens[98]) and only received power later in November of 66 AD (Revelation 17:12).

---

[97] Josephus, War, 2.17.10-2.18.1.

[98] Stevens, The Final Decade, 84.

- The ten Jewish generals handed over their power to the beast (Revelation 17:13) by "surrendering" to the Romans.
- They reigned for "one hour" (Revelation 17:12) or just over three and a half years, short reigns for kings.
- The ten Jewish generals sat upon the sea beast or Rome (Revelation 13:1; 17:3), hated their Jewish brethren who were loyal to Rome, helped destroy Jerusalem (Revelation 17:16), and worked with Rome to persecute Christianity (Revelation 13:7; 17:6; 19:19).
- The ten Jewish generals were thrown into a literal lake of fire (Revelation 19:20) during the siege of Jerusalem, although some later faced their deaths in Rome.

The ten Jewish generals elected in 66 AD fulfilled all the prophecies concerning the ten horns of the sea beast.

Following the vision of the sea beast and its ten horns, John saw a vision of a beast coming out of the land. Who was this beast?

Chapter 13
The Land Beast

The second beast from the land was the Behemoth (1 Enoch 60:7-8; 4 Ezra 6:49-51; Job 40:15-24). The Behemoth was closely associated with the Leviathan, or sea beast, in end-time prophecy.

> Revelation 13:11-15 (ESV) Then I saw another beast rising
> out of the earth. It had two horns like a lamb and it spoke
> like a dragon. 12 It exercises all the authority of the first
> beast in its presence, and makes the earth and its
> inhabitants worship the first beast, whose mortal wound
> was healed. 13 It performs great signs, even making fire
> come down from heaven to earth in front of people, 14 and
> by the signs that it is allowed to work in the presence of the
> beast it deceives those who dwell on earth, telling them to
> make an image for the beast that was wounded by the
> sword and yet lived. 15 And it was allowed to give breath to
> the image of the beast, so that the image of the beast might
> even speak and might cause those who would not worship
> the image of the beast to be slain.

(For information on the mark of the beast, see "Chapter 14 A Dramatic End".)

History strongly indicates that the Roman empire under the resurrected Flavian dynasty (Vespasian and Titus) was the beast from the land. The symbology of the above passage and others concerning the land beast will be explained in the following sections.

Two Horns: Vespasian and Titus

The land beast was the resurrected Roman empire under Vespasian and Titus. Horns in apocalyptic language often represent rulers (Daniel 7:24). The Behemoth had two horns like a lamb (Revelation 13:11). The horns of the land beast were rulers, Vespasian and Titus, who reigned as joint Caesars.[99]

The Behemoth entered the story by rising out of the earth (Revelation 13:11). The "earth" in Revelation was usually a symbol for Israel. It was in Judea that Vespasian and Titus were first made emperor according to Josephus.[100] Rising out of the earth was also an allusion to a body being resurrected.

The Resurrection of Rome

After having been sent by Nero to subdue Jerusalem, Vespasian and Titus returned to Rome to rescue it from its civil war.[101] During the Roman civil war, which started with Nero's death (June 9, 68 AD), the Romans believed their empire would not survive.[102] Thus, the "throne of the beast" was "plunged into darkness" (Revelation 16:10). The peace and order established

---

99 Dio, Roman History, 66.1, https://penelope.uchicago.edu/Thayer/E/Roman/Texts/Cassius_Dio/65*.html.

100 Josephus, War, 6.5.4.

101 Josephus, War, 4.10-11.

102 4 Ezra 12:18; Tacitus, The History, 1.2, 1.3, 1.11, http://www.perseus.tufts.edu/hopper/text?doc=Tac.+Hist.+1.11&fromdoc=Perseus%3Atext%3A1999.02.0080; Josephus, War, 4.10.2, 4.11.5.

during Vespasian and Titus' reign were like a resurrection of the empire.

The Behemoth Came After Nero

The Behemoth could not be Nero. The Behemoth made the earth "worship the first beast" (Revelation 13:12 [ESV]) "who was wounded by the sword and yet lived" (Revelation 13:14 [ESV]). Because Nero was the head of the first beast that was wounded by a sword, the Behemoth arrived on the scene after Nero, the head, was wounded.

Behemoth, the False Prophet

Throughout the book, Revelation consistently refers to the first sea beast without qualifiers simply as "the beast." Moreover, the book always describes the land beast or Behemoth as "the False Prophet." (Revelation 16:13; 19:20; 20:10).

Nowhere does Revelation introduce a character by the name of "the False Prophet." When such a title first appears in the book (Revelation 16:13), it refers to a character previously introduced.

Only the Behemoth, or land beast, matches the description of the False Prophet.

> Revelation 13:14 (ESV) and by the **signs** that it [the land beast] is allowed to work **in the presence** of the beast [sea beast] it **deceives** those who dwell on earth, telling them to make an **image for the beast** that was wounded by the sword and yet lived.

> Revelation 19:20 (ESV) And the beast was captured, and with it the **false prophet** who **in its presence** had done the **signs** by which he **deceived** those who had received the mark of the beast and those who worshiped **its image**.

The land beast worked signs in the presence of the sea beast, deceiving those on the earth to worship an image of the sea beast. The False Prophet likewise worked signs in the presence of the sea beast and deceived those who worshiped the image of the sea beast and received its mark. Therefore, the Behemoth was the False Prophet.

Additionally, the Behemoth was described as a "lamb" that "spoke like a dragon" (Revelation 13:11). The lamb was a picture of the Messiah (John 1:29; Revelation 12:11; 17:14; 21:27; 22:3). The fact that it spoke like a dragon, shows that it was a false Messiah. In the next section, evidence will be presented to show Vespasian satisfactorily fulfilled that role.

Vespasian, the False Messiah

Vespasian performed great signs and saw himself as the Jewish Messiah. In one instance, he spat on a blind man and restored his sight; in another, he stomped on a man's diseased, withered hand, which restored it.[103] He called himself the Messiah to legitimize his reign.[104] His reign was preceded by other omens and false signs.

---

[103] Tacitus, The History, 4.81, http://www.perseus.tufts.edu/hopper/text?doc=Tac.+Hist.+4.81&fromdoc=Perseus%3Atext%3A1999.02.0080.

[104] Tacitus The History, 5.13, http://www.perseus.tufts.edu/hopper/text?doc=Tac.+Hist.+5.13&fromdoc=Perseus%3Atext%3A1999.02.0080.

Cassius Dio said a comet was seen, the moon suffered two eclipses in the same week, two suns, one weak and one strong, were in the sky at once, giant footprints were seen in the capital, and the temple of Jupiter opened itself, causing its guards to faint out of fear.[105] Tacitus wrote of other miracles, such as an apparition of superhuman size suddenly emerging from the Chapel of Juno. On a sunny, windless day, the statue of Julius Caesar turned around to face east instead of west, symbolizing how Vespasian, who was in Judea to the east, would supplant Vitellius from the west. An ox spoke, there were strange animal births, and numerous other signs and wonders occurred.[106] These signs were interpreted favorably for Vespasian's claim to the throne and helped him win the allegiance of the Roman empire.

Armies Gathered for War

After false signs helped Vespasian become Caesar, he instructed Roman armies to gather for war against Jerusalem, thus fulfilling the prophecy that the False Prophet used false signs to gather armies for battle (Revelation 16:12-16). Before the siege of Jerusalem, these armies gathered at what historians suppose is Armageddon, the Mountain of

---

[105] Dio, Roman History, 64.8.1-2, https://penelope.uchicago.edu/Thayer/e/roman/texts/cassius_dio/64*.html.

[106] Tacitus, The History, 1.86, http://www.perseus.tufts.edu/hopper/text?doc=Perseus%3Atext%3A1999.02.0080%3Abook%3D1%3Achapter%3D86.

Megiddo,[107] or Mount Carmel, before continuing to Jerusalem. Revelation did not say a battle happened there, only that the armies gathered in this place to prepare for war.

Fire from Heaven

Vespasian made Titus the general of the Roman armies and sent him to subdue Jerusalem. Thus, Titus fulfilled the prophecy that the beast would "hate the prostitute" (Revelation 17:16).

The Behemoth performed great signs, even bringing fire down from heaven (Revelation 13:13). Before the temple's destruction in Jerusalem, the Romans threw white stones mixed with fire, a talent in weight, into the city. Josephus described these stones best in a similar siege at Jotapata, saying:

> At the same time such engines as were intended for that purpose threw at once lances upon them with a great noise, **and stones of the weight of a talent were thrown by the engines that were prepared for that purpose, together with fire**, and a vast multitude of arrows, which made the wall so dangerous, that the Jews durst not only come upon it, but durst not come to those parts within the walls which were reached by the engines.[108]

Titus acted as an extension of the False Prophet when he made "fire come down from heaven" under the orders of Vespasian.

---

[107] Morais, Daniel. n.d. "Revelation 16: A Preterist Commentary." Revelation Revolution Foundation. Accessed December 10, 2022. https://www.revelationrevolution.org/revelation-16-a-preterist-commentary/.

[108] Josephus, War, 3.7.9.

Worship of the Beast

Vespasian and Titus wielded all the authority and power of Rome, the first beast.

> Revelation 13:12 (ESV) It [the land beast] exercises all the authority of the first beast [the sea beast] in its presence, and makes the earth and its inhabitants worship the first beast, whose mortal wound was healed.

The Roman legions worshiped the images of Caesar and Rome, depicted on their flags and ensigns.[109] Morais says the image of Rome was called the "Aquila," and the image of the reigning emperor was called the "Imago." Josephus said the Romans worshiped and offered sacrifices to these images in the Jewish temple after the war.[110] The Jews who failed to do the same were killed.[111] In this way, the land beast made those who dwelt upon the earth worship the sea beast whose wound had been healed (Revelation 13:12,14).

The Image Spoke

The Romans worshiped the image of Vespasian during the siege of Jerusalem, but Revelation 13:15 says the land beast (Titus and Vespasian) made the image come alive and caused it to speak.

---

[109] Morais, Revelation 13: A Preterist Commentary, https://www.revelationrevolution.org/revelation-13-a-preterist-commentary/.

[110] Josephus, War, 6.6.1.

[111] Josephus, War, 6.6.1-6.9.4.

> Revelation 13:15 (ESV) And it [the land beast] was allowed to give breath to the image of the beast [the sea beast], so that the image of the beast might even speak and might cause those who would not worship the image of the beast to be slain.

Titus and Vespasian reigned jointly as Caesars and shared the same name, "Titus Flavius Vespasianus." Hence, Titus was the local living embodiment of the image of Vespasian giving it voice.

The Destruction of the False Prophet

Recall that the False Prophet was captured and thrown into the lake of fire (Revelation 19:20). The lake of fire was a punishment awaiting the wicked in the afterlife.

Vespasian got sick and died after seeing a falling star in 79 AD.[112] Two months later, Mount Vesuvius erupted covering two cities of Rome in a lake of fire.[113] Titus died suddenly of a fever just two years later after thunder was heard from a clear sky.[114]

Summary

Vespasian and Titus fulfilled all the prophecies of the land beast or Behemoth.

---

[112] Dio, Roman History, 66.17, https://penelope.uchicago.edu/Thayer/e/roman/texts/cassius_dio/66*.html.

[113] Dio, Roman History, 66.22-24.

[114] Suetonius, Titus, 10-11, https://penelope.uchicago.edu/Thayer/E/Roman/Texts/Suetonius/12Caesars/Titus*.html.

- Vespasian and Titus became the two horns of the Behemoth (Revelation 13:11) when they took the throne of Rome as joint Caesars.
- The reign of Vespasian and Titus was a resurrection of the Roman empire from its death and fulfilled the prophecy that the Behemoth came out of the land (Revelation 13:11).
- Vespasian and Titus made the world worship the first beast, Rome and its Caesars, that was wounded and lived (Revelation 13:12,14).
- The Behemoth had two horns like a lamb but spoke like a dragon (Revelation 13:11), a clear picture of a false Messiah (John 1:29; Revelation 12:11; 17:14; 21:27; 22:3). Vespasian called himself the Jewish Messiah and performed many false signs to legitimize his reign in Rome.
- The Behemoth was later referred to as the False Prophet (Revelation 13:14; 16:13; 19:20; 20:10). Vespasian likewise used false miracles and signs to take the throne and make the earth worship Rome.
- After becoming Caesar, Vespasian gathered his armies against Judea at Armageddon, fulfilling Revelation 16:12-16.
- Like the land beast, Vespasian, acting through Titus, brought fire from heaven (Revelation 13:13) down upon Jerusalem during the siege.

- Titus forced the world to worship the image of Rome and its Caesar, depicted on the Roman flags and ensigns (Revelation 13:12,14-15).
- Titus and Vespasian were joint Caesars and shared the same name, "Titus Flavius Vespasianus;" hence, Titus was the living embodiment of the image of Vespasian and gave the images of him a voice (Revelation 13:15).
- Vespasian and Titus both suffered in the lake of fire (Revelation 19:20), a punishment of the afterlife, when they suddenly died of a sickness after a comet was seen, Mount Vesuvius erupted, and thunder sounded from a clear sky.

The above points and previous chapters demonstrate that first century Rome and apostate Jerusalem were the primary villains in Revelation. They teamed up against Christianity and were both thrown into a lake of fire.

Now that the characters of Revelation have been identified, some of the events in Revelation can be understood.

Chapter 14
A Dramatic End

Revelation's prophecies are filled with seemingly world-ending language. Although apocalyptic language is metaphorical in nature, it does point to a literal reality. The scope and intensity of the signs and tragedies in the first century deserved such language to describe them.

The 666 Mark of the Beast

> Revelation 13:16 (ESV) causes all, both small and great, both rich and poor, both free and slave, to be **marked** on the right hand or the forehead

The mark of Revelation 13:16 had both a spiritual and physical component. The spiritual mark proved whom one belonged to or whom one served (Exodus 13:15-16). In Ezekiel, those who sighed and groaned over the abominations committed in Jerusalem were "marked" (Ezekiel 9:3-6).

Those loyal to Rome were marked spiritually with the beast's mark (Revelation 13:16). The 144,000 saints loyal to God were marked spiritually on their foreheads (Ephesians 4:30; Revelation 7:3; 14:1). Christian Jews would naturally contrast receiving the mark of the beast "on their foreheads or their hands" with failing to keep God's laws and their testimony about Christ in their thoughts or their deeds (Exodus 13:9; Deuteronomy 6:4-8; Revelation 14:11-12).

In Deuteronomy 6:4-8, God illustrated the importance of remembering and obeying his commands by telling them to make his words and commandments a sign on their hand and frontlets between their eyes. He did not intend for Jews to literally walk around with the Mosaic law written on their hands and between their eyes.

> Deuteronomy 6:4-8 (ESV) Hear, O Israel: The Lord our God, the Lord is one. You shall love the Lord your God with all your heart and with all your soul and with all your might. And these words that I command you today shall be on your heart. You shall teach them diligently to your children, and shall talk of them when you sit in your house, and when you walk by the way, and when you lie down, and when you rise. You shall bind them **as a sign on your hand**, and they shall be **as frontlets between your eyes**.

Having God's laws as a sign on the hand and forehead meant to think about and do the things God commanded.

The physical component of the mark was the Roman coins and deeds with Caesar's image that the Romans forced the Jews to use if they wanted to buy or sell.

> Revelation 13:17 (ESV) no one can buy or sell unless he has the mark, that is, the name of the beast or the number of its name

Before the start of the war in 66 AD, the Jews created their own coins without graven images on them. The second commandment in the Mosaic law forbade the Jews to bow down, serve, or create carved images in the likeness of anything in the heavens, earth, or waters (Exodus 20:4; Deuteronomy 5:8). Roman coins were a clear violation of this commandment. Morais describes one of the coins the Romans forced the Jews to use after the fall of Jerusalem in 70 AD:

115

After the fall of Jerusalem in A.D. 70 all Jews who remained in Judaea, Jerusalem and the rest of Israel in addition to those who were exiled throughout Rome were forced to use Roman money marked with the name and image of the beast [Caesar]. Thus after the fall of Jerusalem it would have been impossible to buy or sell anywhere in the Roman Empire without the mark of the beast. Thus it is interesting to note that a coin issued in A.D. 72 is marked with the following legend around Vespasian's head: IMP CAES VESP AVG P M COS IIII. If one were to transliterate this inscription into Hebrew characters it would read as follows ymp qys wsp 'wg p m kws d.148 The sum total of the

[115] The legend above this coin reads, "IMP CAES VESP AVG P M COS IIII." The Latin alphabet originally did not have unique characters for the vowel "U" or the consonant "V" and thus rendered "U" and "V" as a "V".

> numerical values of these Hebrew characters adds up to 666 in explicit fulfillment of Revelation 13:17-18.[116]

Additionally, when people worshiped Nero, they "received a certificate or mark of approval - charagma, the same word used in Revelation 13:16."[117] Richard Anthony says,

> All those under the jurisdiction of Rome were required by law to publicly proclaim their allegiance to Caesar by burning a pinch of incense and declaring, 'Caesar is Lord'. Upon compliance with this law, the people were given a papyrus document called a 'libellus', which they were required to present when either stopped by the Roman police or attempting to engage in commerce in the Roman marketplace, increasing the difficulty of 'buying or selling' without this mark.[118]

In many ancient languages, including Latin, Greek, and Hebrew, the letters also served as numbers. The dual meanings of these letters created an art form in that day called cryptograms or gematria, where the letters of a name were added to encode and decode an individual's identity. The angel said the number "666," also "616" in some manuscripts, was the number for a man (Revelation 13:18).

> Revelation 13:18 (ESV) This calls for wisdom: let the one who has understanding calculate the number of the beast,

---

[116] Morais, Revelation 13: A Preterist Commentary, https://www.revelationrevolution.org/revelation-13-a-preterist-commentary/.

[117] Pate, C. M., and Calvin B. Haines. 1995. Doomsday Delusions: What's Wrong with Predictions about the End of the World. N.p.: InterVasity Press.

[118] Anthony, Richard. n.d. "The Mark Of The Beast." ecclesia.org. Accessed December 10, 2022. http://www.ecclesia.org/truth/beast.html.

for it is the number of a man, and his number is 666 [some manuscripts say 616]

Kenneth Gentry illustrates that the sum of each letter of the Hebrew spelling of Nero Caesar adds up to 666.[119] When transliterated into Hebrew, the Latin form of Nero Caesar also totals 616.[120] Nero's constituents also called him a beast.[121]

Nero was the head of the Hydra that was severed, but as described in "Chapter 11 The Sea Beast," two heads grew up in its place. Brian Jones says Titus and Vespasian went by the joint title, "Titus Flavius Vespasianus Augustus."[122] When translated into Hebrew, this title also adds up to 666.[123] Hence, they inherit the 666 value of the first head.

Recall that the ten horns of the sea beast were ten Jewish generals, showing that the sea beast was not exclusively Roman. Perhaps the 666 mark of the beast also pointed to a Jewish entity. Many scholars have suggested this, noting that King Solomon was said to collect "666" talents of gold per year (1 Kings 10:14; 2 Chronicles 9:13), and that Solomon built the

---

119 Gentry, Kenneth L. 2010. Before Jerusalem Fell: Dating the Book of Revelation. N.p.: Victorious Hope Publishing, 193-219, 203.

120 Gentry, 203.

121 Gentry.

122 Jones, Brian, and Robert Milns, 2002, Suetonius: The Flavian Emperors, A Historical Commentary, London: Bristol Classic Press, 90, cited in Duncan W. McKenzie, PH.D., The Antichrist and the Second Coming: A Preterist Examination, vol. II (United States: Xulon Press, 2012), 191.

123 Beckwith, Isbon T. 2001. The Apocalypse of John. N.p.: Wipf & Stock Publishers, 645.

temple, where those rejecting Jesus continued to worship. Such a view would be consistent with the idea that symbols in Revelation sometimes describe more than one thing.

The mark of the beast and its number represented Nero, Vespasian & Titus, and the coins, libellus and charagmas, which the Romans forced the Jews to use if they wanted to buy and sell. One may theorize that it represented a Jewish entity, as well.

Thrown Into Darkness

In the previous chapter, it was noted that Rome fell into darkness during the civil war following Nero's suicide. However, Rome was literally cast into darkness when Mount Vesuvius erupted. In 79 AD, smoke from the volcano hid the sun and stars all the way to Egypt, and Rome fell into darkness.[124] An unprecedented plague followed among the Romans, likely as a result of the acid rain from the volcano.[125]

> Revelation 16:10-11 (ESV) The fifth angel poured out his bowl on the throne of the beast, and its kingdom was plunged into darkness. People gnawed their tongues in anguish 11 and cursed the God of heaven for their pain and sores. They did not repent of their deeds.

---

[124] Dio, Roman History, 66.22-23, https://penelope.uchicago.edu/Thayer/e/roman/texts/cassius_dio/66*.html.

[125]Dio, Roman History, 66.23.5, https://penelope.uchicago.edu/Thayer/e/roman/texts/cassius_dio/66*.html; Tranquillus, Caius S. 1914. The Life of Titus, The Lives of the Twelve Caesars. Translated by John C. Rolfe. N.p.: Loeb Classical Library edition. https://penelope.uchicago.edu/Thayer/E/Roman/Texts/Suetonius/12Caesars/Titus*.html, 8.3.

Jewish zealots also endured a dark period before and during the siege of Jerusalem. They divided themselves into three factions[126] and burned each other's food supplies. Josephus said "pestilential destruction" came upon them, likely from the unburied dead that filled the city.[127] Just as Deuteronomy 28:27 prophesied, Jerusalem suffered the sixth plague of boils in Exodus. Thus, painful sores came on those who bore the mark of the beast (Revelation 16:2).

Signs in the Heavens and Earth

Jesus and Joel prophesied that signs would appear in the stars and on earth before the destruction of Jerusalem (Joel 2:28-32).

> Luke 21:25-26 (ESV) "And **there will be signs in sun and moon and stars**, and on the earth distress of nations in perplexity because of the roaring of the sea and the waves, 26 people fainting with fear and with foreboding of what is coming on the world. For the powers of the heavens will be shaken.

> Acts 2:19-20 (WEB) **I will show wonders in the sky above, and signs on the earth beneath**: blood, and fire, and billows of smoke. 20 The sun will be turned into darkness, and the moon into blood, before the great and glorious day of the Lord comes.

> Matthew 24:29 (NIV) "'the sun will be darkened, and the moon will not give its light; the stars will fall from the sky, and the heavenly bodies will be shaken.'

---

126 Josephus, War, 5.1.1.

127 Josephus, War, 6.9.3.

In fulfillment of Jesus' and Joel's words, several cosmic events did occur in the skies before the Jewish war of 66-70 AD. Cassius Dio wrote about an event in 69 AD:

> [E]vil omens occurred. A comet was seen, and the moon, contrary to precedent, appeared to suffer two eclipses, being obscured on the fourth and on the seventh day. Also people saw two suns at once, one in the west weak and pale, and one in the east brilliant and powerful.[128]

The above account seems to also be a fulfillment of Isaiah 30:26.

> Isaiah 30:26 (ESV) Moreover, the light of the moon will be as the light of the sun, and the light of the sun will be sevenfold, as the light of seven days...

Sepher Yosippon also described miraculous events during Passover 66 AD.

> Now it happened after this that there was seen from above over the Holy of Holies for the whole night the outline of a man's face, the like of whose beauty had never been seen in all the land, and his appearance was quite awesome.[129]

Josephus also recorded remarkable signs in the stars and on earth, most of which occurred during Passover, April 28 - May 5 66 AD (Nisan 14-21).

---

[128] Dio, 64.8.1-2, https://penelope.uchicago.edu/Thayer/e/roman/texts/cassius_dio/64*.html.

[129]Yosippon, 87.

Thus were the miserable people persuaded by these deceivers, and such as belied God himself. While they did not attend, nor give credit to the signs that were so evident, and did so plainly foretel their future desolation. But like men infatuated, without either eyes to see, or minds to consider, did not regard the denunciations that God made to them. Thus there was a star, resembling a sword, which stood over the city: and a comet, that continued a whole year. (15) Thus also before the Jews rebellion, and before those commotions which preceded the war, when the people were come in great crouds to the feast of unleavened bread, on the eighth day of the month Xanthicus, [Nisan,] [April 28] (16) and at the ninth hour of the night, so great a light shone round the altar, and the holy house, that it appeared to be bright day time. Which light lasted for half an hour. This light seemed to be a good sign to the unskilful: but was so interpreted by the sacred scribes, as to portend those events that followed immediately upon it. At the same festival also an heifer [female cow], as she was led by the High-priest to be sacrificed, brought forth a lamb, in the midst of the temple. Moreover the eastern gate of the inner [court of the] temple,9 which was of brass, and vastly heavy, and had been with difficulty shut by twenty men, and rested upon a basis armed with iron, and had bolts fastened very deep into the firm floor; which was there made of one intire stone: was seen to be opened of its own accord, about the sixth hour of the night. Now those that kept watch in the temple came hereupon running to the captain of the temple, and told him of it: who then came up thither: and, not without great difficulty, was able to shut the gate again. This also appeared to the vulgar to be a very happy prodigy:

> as if God did thereby open them the gate of happiness. But the men of learning understood it, that the security of their holy house was dissolved of its own accord: and that the gate was opened for the advantage of their enemies. So these publickly declared that this signal foreshewed the desolation that was coming upon them.[130]

The above signs were a clear fulfillment of Joel's prophecy of "wonders in the sky above, and signs on the earth beneath."

The Four Angels at Euphrates

Sometimes the Bible calls humans "angels" (2 Chronicles 36:15-16; Haggai 1:13; Malachi 3:1; Matthew 11:10; 24:31; Luke 7:24; 9:52; 1 Timothy 3:16; Revelation 2:1,8,12,18; 3:1,7,14; 21:17). In the passage below, the four angels represented the four generals of the Roman legions bound at the Euphrates before the Jewish war.

> Revelation 9:14-15 (ESV) saying to the sixth angel who had the trumpet, "Release the four angels who are bound at the great river Euphrates." 15 So the four angels, who had been prepared for the hour, the day, the month, and the year, were released to kill a third of mankind.

Concerning the four angels mentioned in the above passage, Morais writes:

> During the siege of Jerusalem in A.D. 70, there were four Roman legions under Titus' command: Legio V Macedonica, Legio X Fretensis, Legio XII Fulminata, and Legio XV Apollinaris. The four angels bound at the

[130] Josephus, War, 6.5.3, http://penelope.uchicago.edu/josephus/war-6.html.

Euphrates appears to refer to the generals of these four legions. The fact that these four legions are said to be bound at the Euphrates also appears to be an historical easter egg as Titus' four legions were all bound at the Euphrates just three years before the outbreak of the Jewish revolt. In A.D. 63 at the conclusion of the Roman-Parthian War all four of Titus' Roman legions were stationed at the Euphrates.47 In A.D. 63 XII Fulminata was stationed in Zeugma48 at the banks of the Euphrates.49 X Fretensis was left to guard Cappadocia again presumably to guard the Parthian boarder at the Euphrates. And that year V Macedonica and XV Apollinaris crossed the Euphrates into Armenia in response to the Parthian threat.[131]

A third of humankind was killed during the Jewish war in a unique manner. After multitudes of Jews came from all the nations into Jerusalem for Passover, the Romans locked them inside and began their siege. Josephus says a significant number of people, "not fewer in number than three millions," visited Jerusalem during Passover at the start of the war.[132] If the same number attended the feast in 70 AD, a likely scenario, those killed in Jerusalem, "eleven hundred thousand" or over one million, would be one-third of its population. Josephus wrote:

> Now the number (26) of those that were carried captive, during this whole war, was collected to be ninety-seven thousand. As was the number of those that perished during

---

[131]Morais, Revelation 9, https://www.revelationrevolution.org/revelation-9-a-preterist-commentary-who-is-apollyon/.

[132] Josephus, War, 2.14.3.

Revelation 11:13 (ESV) And at that hour there was a great earthquake, and **a tenth of the city fell. Seven thousand people were killed in the earthquake**, and the rest were terrified and gave glory to the God of heaven.

The Sea of Blood

Every living thing in the sea died when the second bowl of wrath was poured upon the sea.

Revelation 16:3 (ESV) The second angel poured out his bowl into the sea, and it became like the blood of a corpse, and every living thing died that was in the sea.

On July 5, 67 AD (Tamuz 4), the people of Joppa were slaughtered near the Mediterranean Sea. Josephus wrote:

"[T]he sea was bloody a long way, and the maritime parts were full of dead bodies."[139]

Later, on September 6, 67 AD (Elul 8), Jews from Taricheae were killed in the sea of Galilee, and Josephus said:

"[O]ne might then see the lake all bloody, and full of dead bodies, for not one of them escaped."[140]

Furthermore, when Mount Vesuvius erupted in 79 AD, Cassius Dio said all fish were killed.

While this was going on, an inconceivable quantity of ashes was blown out, which covered both sea and land and filled all the air. It wrought much injury of various kinds, as

[139] Josephus, War, 3.9.3, http://penelope.uchicago.edu/josephus/war-3.html.

[140] Josephus, War, 3.10.9, http://penelope.uchicago.edu/josephus/war-3.html.

> chance befell, to men and farms and cattle, and in particular **it destroyed all fish** and birds.[141]

Similarly, the third bowl of wrath turned the rivers to blood, and people were given blood to drink.

> Revelation 16:4-6 (ESV) The third angel poured out his bowl into the rivers and the springs of water, and they became blood. 5 And I heard the angel in charge of the waters say, "Just are you, O Holy One, who is and who was, for you brought these judgments. 6 For they have shed the blood of saints and prophets, and you have given them blood to drink. It is what they deserve!"

On February 27, 68 AD (Adar 5), the Jews were slaughtered in the Jordan River so that it flowed red with blood. Josephus wrote:

> And this because, not only the whole country through which they fled was filled with slaughter, and Jordan could not be passed over by reason of the dead bodies that were in it; but because the lake Asphaltitis [Dead Sea] was also full of dead bodies, that were carried down into it by the river.[142]

Adam Maarschalk notes that many Jews slaughtered by the Romans were pushed into the water[143] and drowned. He explains that when someone drowns, their desire to breathe underwater becomes so strong that they swallow water into

---

141 Dio, Roman History, 66.23.3, https://penelope.uchicago.edu/Thayer/e/roman/texts/cassius_dio/66*.html.

142 Josephus, War, 4.7.6, http://penelope.uchicago.edu/josephus/war-4.html.

143 Josephus, War, 4.7.5.

their lungs. So when the Jews were drowned this way, they were literally drinking blood to fulfill this prophecy.

Summary

The tragic and dramatic events of the first century deserve Revelation's terrible, world-ending language.

1. The Romans demanded the Jews worship Caesar and forced them to use Roman currency and deeds if they wanted to buy and sell in fulfillment of Revelation 13:16-17. Nero, Vespasian, Titus, and the coins and deeds that depicted them added up to 666 in fulfillment of Revelation 13:18.

2. When Mount Vesuvius erupted in 79 AD, it literally threw Rome into darkness and brought painful pestilence upon its residents in fulfillment of Revelation 16:10-11.

3. Josephus, Sepher Yosippon, and Cassius Dio recorded miraculous events in the stars before and during the war of the Jews in fulfillment of Luke 21:25-26.

4. The four angels from the Euphrates were the four Roman generals who killed a third of the Jewish inhabitants of the city during the siege in fulfillment of Revelation 9:14-15.

5. The Romans cast white hailstones weighing a talent each on Jerusalem in fulfillment of Revelation 16:21. When the Romans destroyed the temple, approximately

seven thousand Jews were killed and a literal tenth of the city fell in fulfillment of Revelation 11:13.

6. The sea and streams were filled with blood and dead bodies during the war in fulfillment of Revelation 16:3-6.

Reading about the Jewish war was a gut-wrenching and challenging experience. Truly the end of the Old Covenant deserved such dramatic prophecies to describe the terrible events that occurred.

Christians today can find relief in knowing that this prophesied judgment is past.

Chapter 15
The Millennium End

It was demonstrated in Chapter 8 that the Millennium was expected to end soon. How were the prophecies below fulfilled?

> Revelation 20:7-10 (NIV) When the thousand years are over, Satan will be released from his prison 8 and will go out to deceive the nations in the four corners of the earth—Gog and Magog—and to gather them for battle. In number they are like the sand on the seashore. 9 They marched across the breadth of the earth and surrounded the camp of God's people, the city he loves.

First-century, unbelieving Jerusalem killed the Messiah; it should not be surprising that they deserved a major role in the book of Revelation.

Revelation called unbelieving Jerusalem "Egypt," "Sodom," and "Babylon" (Matthew 23:30-38; Revelation 11:8; 18:21,24) because they acted as enemies of God's new people, the church.

Accordingly, Gog is best identified as apostate Jerusalem, and Magog represents Rome. Revelation says Gog and Magog came against "the camp of God's people" (Revelation 20:9). Frequently, these Jews persecuted Christians and likely even inspired the Neronian persecution. Stevens, in his book *The Final Decade*, writes,

> [Philip] Schaff sums up the matter well when he says: "It is not unlikely that in this (as in all previous persecutions, and often afterwards) the fanatical Jews, enraged by the rapid progress of Christianity, and anxious to avert suspicion from themselves, stirred up the people against the hated Galileans, and that the heathen Romans fell with double fury on these supposed half Jews, disowned by their own strange brethren" (as both Ewald and Renan have suggested). [Schaff, Hist. of Christian Church] In order to deflect accusations away from himself, Nero accused the Christians. The Jews in Rome 152 (using their good relationship with Nero's "religious" wife Poppaea, Antiq. 20.195) may have helped Nero concoct this accusation. They had both "motive" and "opportunity." Eusebius quotes Justin Martyr as saying that the Jews throughout the Roman empire had more than once circulated such false slanders against the Christians in order to prejudice the Roman authorities against them. [Euseb. Eccl. Hist. 4.18] He quotes Melito also about such Jewish "informers." [Euseb. Eccl. Hist. 4.26] Another tidbit of history that supports these

> suspicions is the fact that the Jewish quarter of the city (region 14), which lay across the Tiber river to the southwest, escaped the damaging fires. Therefore, some Romans suspected the Jews of lighting the fires, since their quarter of the city was virtually untouched. However, since Nero's "religious" wife was somewhat friendly toward the Jewish people, Nero may have spared their part of the city from the torch. This raises the question about whether the Jews may have known about the burning of the city in advance, or simply were spared because of their friendly relations with Nero, and their trans-Tiber location. However, since many of the Christians were Jewish, and lived in the Jewish quarter of the city, it would have been easy for the Jews to divert the suspicion against them over to the Christians.[144]

Faithless Jerusalem and Rome worked together against Christianity. Tom Mills, writing in an end times study group on Facebook, says:

> Did you know in the Septuagint, in the story of Esther, Haaman, the villain of the story that tried to kill all the Jews by the king's decree, is called a "Gogite"? The Hebrew scriptures say Agagite, but in the LXX it's Gogite. I find that very enlightening! In the same way that Babylon from the OT [Old Testament] is used to describe Israel in the NT, I think that perhaps it is the same thing with the Gogites applying to some villain in the New too![145]

---

144 Stevens, The Final Decade, 152-153.

145 Tom Mills' Facebook comment. Accessed October 28, 2021. https://www.facebook.com/groups/323994044837028/posts/1024047801498312/.

Robert Cruickshank, in a pre-publication transcript about Gog and Magog, building on the work of Gary DeMar[146] and James Jordan,[147] discovers a powerful connection between Ezekiel, Esther, and Revelation. While he brings several compelling lines of evidence, an attempt will be made to briefly summarize his point.

John frequently reminded his audience of stories from their past to encourage them in their present situations. Jezebel (Revelation 2:20), Egypt (Revelation 11:8), Sodom (Revelation 11:8), and Babylon (Revelation 14:8; 16:19; 17:5; 18:2,10,21) were brought to mind to tell God's people, "Remember how God delivered us from these people? He will do the same now in the same way!"

The prophecy of Gog and Magog in Ezekiel 38-39 was fulfilled in the Book of Esther almost ninety years later.

- Gog devised an evil plan against Jews living in unwalled villages (Ezekiel 38:10-11); Haman devised an evil plan against the Jews, who at that unique moment in history, were living in unwalled villages (Esther 9:19).

---

[146] DeMar, Gary. 2016. The Gog and Magog End-Time Alliance, Israel, Russia, and Syria in Bible Prophecy. Powder Springs, Georgia: American Vision Press;
DeMar, Gary. 2008. Why the End of the World is Not in Your Future, Identifying the Gog-Magog Alliance. Powder Springs, Georgia: American Vision Press.

[147] Jordan, James B. 1995. Esther in the Midst of Covenant History. Niceville on the Bayou of the Bog, Florida: Biblical Horizons.

- Gog wanted to "seize spoil" and "carry off plunder" from Israel (Ezekiel 38:12); Haman wanted to "seize their possessions as plunder" (Esther 3:13).
- Gog comes to take Israel's "silver and gold" (Ezekiel 38:13); Haman promised to pay off Persia's treasuries with "silver" plundered from the Jews (Esther 3:9,11, 4:7).
- The burial place for Gog was called "Hamon-Gog" (Ezekiel 39:11), bringing to mind Haman.

The book of Esther records that in the twelfth year of King Xerxes (Esther 3:7), or spring of 474 BC, Haman conspired with the King of Persia to wipe out the Jews. However, the plan backfired, King Xerxes turned on Haman, and the Jews were delivered.

Similarly, in 64 AD, the unbelieving Jews conspired with Roman Caesar Nero to wipe out the Christians. In the end, the plan backfired; Rome turned on the Jews, and God's people, the Christians, were delivered from their persecutors.

Cruickshank's discoveries are invaluable to understanding the book of Revelation, and it is much appreciated that his pre-publication research was permitted to be shared here.

Satan Released

Christian persecution existed in small doses before 64 AD. However, the Roman empire was ambivalent towards Christians. Emperor Tiberius had ordered Roman officials not to interfere with the new religion and even tried to legalize Christianity.[148]

Still, in mid-November that year, the Neronian persecution started. The "sword of Caesar" was used against Christians for the first time. Tertullian says,

> Consult your histories; you will there find that Nero was the first who assailed with the imperial sword the Christian sect, making progress then especially at Rome. But we glory in having our condemnation hallowed by the hostility of such a wretch. For any one who knows him, can understand that not except as being of singular excellence did anything bring on it Nero's condemnation.[149]

A fire broke out in Rome, and the Jews incentivized Nero to blame the Christians. Christians were hunted down and subjected to widespread and brutal torture. Notice what Philip Schaff had to say about that time.

> Under this wanton charge of incendiarism, backed by the equally groundless charge of misanthropy and unnatural vice, there began a carnival of blood such as even heathen Rome never saw before or since. **It was the answer of the powers of hell to the mighty preaching of the two chief apostles, which had shaken heathenism to its [foundations]. A "vast multitude" of Christians [were] put**

---

148 Constitutional Rights Foundation. n.d. "Constitutional Rights Foundation." Constitutional Rights Foundation. Accessed January 6, 2023. https://www.crf-usa.org/bill-of-rights-in-action/bria-13-4-b-religious-tolerance-and-persecution-in-the-roman-empire.

149 Tertullian, Apology, 1.5 (3.22), https://www.newadvent.org/fathers/0301.htm.

> **to death in the most shocking manner**. Some were crucified, probably in mockery of the punishment of Christ, some sewed up in the skins of wild beasts and exposed to the voracity of mad dogs in the arena. The satanic tragedy reached its climax at night in the imperial gardens on the slope of the Vatican (which embraced, it is supposed, the present site of the place and church of St. Peter): Christian men and women, covered with pitch or oil or resin, and nailed to posts of pine, were lighted and burned as torches for the amusement of the mob; while Nero, in fantastical dress, figured in a horse race, and displayed his art as charioteer. Burning alive was the ordinary punishment of incendiaries; **but only the cruel ingenuity of this imperial monster, under the inspiration of the devil, could invent such a horrible system of illumination.**[150]

This tribulation of the saints was not limited to Rome but "extended throughout the length and breadth of the Empire." Stevens writes:

> Philip Schaff tells us that Sulpicius Severus (c. 363-425) in his Chronicle (2:28-29) "gives a pretty full account [of the horrors suffered in Rome], but mostly [copied] from Tacitus. Both he and Orosius (c. 375-418, History Against the Pagans 7:7) [were the first to] clearly assert **that Nero extended the persecution to the provinces**." Both of these were Christian writers, and Orosius worked with both Augustine and Jerome.[151]

---

150 Schaff, History of the Christian church, https://ccel.org/ccel/schaff/hcc1/hcc1.i.VI.37.html.

151 Stevens, Final Decade, 152.

He continues:

> But Orazio Marucchi, a Roman Catholic scholar, mentions several Roman and Italian sources who indicate that the Neronic persecution was not just confined to Rome or Italy, but rather:
>
> "...extended throughout the length and breadth of the Empire. The burning of Rome was but a pretext, for the Christians were to be considered as enemies of the human race." [Orazio Marucchi, Manual of Christian Archeology, p. 29][152]

Since the thousand years were coming to a close, the Neronian persecution perfectly fits the release of Satan. He was allowed for a short time to persecute Christians. He "deceived" Rome (Revelation 20:8) into falsely accusing Christians, gathering empire-wide persecution against them.

It was established in Chapter 7 that Satan would wage war against the saints when he was released. Such an event occurred when Nero used the Roman state to persecute Christians.

Rome Destroyed Gog

After Satan attacked the saints, fire came down from heaven to devour Gog and Magog. Satan was thrown into the lake of fire.

> Revelation 20:9-10 (NIV) But fire came down from heaven and devoured them. 10 And the devil, who deceived them, was thrown into the lake of burning sulfur, where the beast

---

[152] Stevens, Final Decade, 155.

> and the false prophet had been thrown. They will be tormented day and night for ever and ever.

Jerusalem, the final personification of Gog, disintegrated in the same way that Gog was prophesied to end. Ezekiel prophesied that Gog would be destroyed by fire.

> Ezekiel 38:21-22 (NIV) I will summon a sword against Gog on all my mountains, declares the Sovereign Lord. Every man's sword will be against his brother. 22 I will execute judgment on him with plague and bloodshed; I will pour down torrents of rain, hailstones and burning sulfur on him and on his troops and on the many nations with him.

When the Jewish war started, Jews who had been living peacefully among Gentiles in cities across the Roman empire broke out in conflict against their Gentile neighbors. Both sides feared the other would be first to strike. Some Jews sided with the Gentiles and killed their brethren. Thousands were killed in various cities in a single day. The wealthy Jews and Jewish zealots also fought among themselves, betraying and destroying each other. Out of their hatred for each other, they refused the honor of letting their brethren bury their dead, leaving piles of dead bodies exposed on the streets and in the houses. This led to a terrible plague that intensified after the Jewish zealot factions destroyed one another's food supply. A dreadful famine followed.

The unbelieving Jews suffered all the curses of the Mosaic law (Deuteronomy 28:58-61). The Romans arrived to find a nation in chaos, brother killing brother, family killing family. Unbelieving Jews from many nations across the Roman empire had gathered in Jerusalem for the annual Jewish feasts and were trapped inside during the war. The Romans rained down burning sulfur and giant rocks on the city, burning it down with fire as Revelation 20:9 prophesied.

Vesuvius Destroyed Magog

A second "fire from heaven" occurred nine years after Jerusalem's destruction. In 79 AD, a massive fire broke out in Rome. It was so severe the Romans believed it was sent by God. At that same time, Cassius Dio wrote of the Abyss opening up and giants roaming the earth and flying through the sky. Could this have been the angels throwing Satan into the lake of fire? Cassius Dio wrote:

> Such is Vesuvius, and these phenomena usually occur there every year. But all the other occurrences that had taken place there in the course of time, however notable, because unusual, they may have seemed to those who on each occasion observed them, nevertheless would be regarded as trivial in comparison with what now happened, even if all had been combined into one. 2 This was what befell. Numbers of huge men quite surpassing any human stature — such creatures, in fact, as the Giants are pictured to have been — appeared, now on the mountain, now in the surrounding country, and again in the cities, wandering over the earth day and night and also flitting through the air. 3 After this fearful droughts and sudden and violent earthquakes occurred, so that the whole plain round about seethed and the summits leaped into the air. There were frequent rumblings, some of them subterranean, that resembled thunder, and some on the surface, that sounded

like bellowings; the sea also joined in the roar and the sky re-echoed it. 4 Then suddenly a portentous crash was heard, as if the mountains were tumbling in ruins; and first huge stones were hurled aloft, rising as high as the very summits, then came a great quantity of fire and endless smoke, so that the whole atmosphere was obscured and the sun was entirely hidden, as if eclipsed. 23 1 Thus day was turned into night and light into darkness. Some thought that the Giants were rising again in revolt (for at this time also many of their forms could be discerned in the smoke and, moreover, a sound as of trumpets was heard), while others believed that the whole universe was being resolved into chaos or fire. 2 Therefore they fled, some from the houses into the streets, others from outside into the houses, now from the sea to the land and now from the land to the sea; for in their excitement they regarded any place where they were not as safer than where they were. 3 While this was going on, an inconceivable quantity of ashes was blown out, which covered both sea and land and filled all the air. It wrought much injury of various kinds, as chance befell, to men and farms and cattle, and in particular it destroyed all fish and birds. Furthermore, it buried two entire cities, Herculaneum and Pompeii, the latter place while its populace was seated in the theatre. 4 Indeed, the amount of dust, taken all together, was so great that some of it reached Africa and Syria and Egypt, and it also reached Rome, filling the air overhead and darkening the sun. 5 There, too, no little fear was occasioned, that lasted for several days, since the people did not know and could not imagine what had happened, but, like those close at hand, believed that the whole world was being turned upside down, that the sun was disappearing into the earth

> and that the earth was being lifted to the sky. These ashes, now, did the Romans no great harm at the time, though later they brought a terrible pestilence upon them.
>
> 24 1 However, a second 5 conflagration [fire], above ground, in the following year spread over very large sections of Rome while Titus was absent in Campania attending to the catastrophe that had befallen that region. 2 It consumed the temple of Serapis, the temple of Isis, the Saepta, the temple of Neptune, the Baths of Agrippa, the Pantheon, the Diribitorium, the theatre of Balbus, the stage building of Pompey's theatre, the Octavian buildings together with their books, 6 and the temple of Jupiter Capitolinus with their surrounding temples. Hence the disaster seemed to be not of human but of divine origin; 3 for anyone can estimate, from the list of buildings that I have given, how many others must have been destroyed.[153]

Perhaps one of the giants roaming around was Satan, and he was cast into Vesuvius. However, that is likely too much imagination. Either way, this event certainly seems to match "fire came down from heaven and devoured them" and occurred within the few short years that Satan had remaining (Revelation 20:3). Cassius Dio himself said,

> Hence the disaster seemed to be not of human but of divine origin;

Those who experienced these events certainly described the heavens and earth as literally shaking.

---

[153] Dio, Roman History, 66.22-24, https://penelope.uchicago.edu/Thayer/e/roman/texts/cassius_dio/66*.html.

> There, too, no little fear was occasioned, that lasted for several days, since the people did not know and could not imagine what had happened, but, like those close at hand, believed that the whole world was being turned upside down, that the sun was disappearing into the earth and that the earth was being lifted to the sky.

Many people who worshiped false gods believed the gods were destroyed at this time. Pliny the Younger, who survived the eruption of Mount Vesuvius, wrote,

> You could hear the wailing of women, the screams of little children, and the shouts of men ; some were trying to find their parents, others their children, others their wives, by calling for them and recognising them by their voices alone. Some were commiserating their own lot, others that of their relatives, while some again prayed for death in sheer terror of dying. Many were lifting up their hands to the gods, **but more were declaring that now there were no more gods**, and that this night would last for ever, and the end of all the world.[154]

Even those loyal to demons believed their deities existed no more, implying that Satan and his demons were cast into the lake of fire at this time.

It was established in a previous chapter that Ezekiel 37-39 parallels Revelation 20. The eruption of Vesuvius destroyed Pompeii and Herculaneum, two cities on the coastlands of Rome in fulfillment of Ezekiel 39:6 and Revelation 20:9:

---

[154] Younger, Pliny t. 1900. Letters. Translated by John B. Firth. R.A.B.Mynors' Latin ed. http://www.attalus.org/info/pliny.html, 6.20, http://www.attalus.org/old/pliny6.html.

> Ezekiel 39:6 (NIV) I will send fire on Magog and on those who live in safety in the coastlands, and they will know that I am the Lord.

> Revelation 20:9 (ESV) but fire came down from heaven and consumed them

By the fire of war, Gog, or faithless Jerusalem was destroyed. Rome, or Magog, was later destroyed by Vesuvius' fire, fulfilling a prophecy from Paul:

> Romans 2:9 (NIV) There will be trouble and distress for every human being who does evil: first for the Jew, then for the Gentile

Furthermore, the Jews and Greeks believed this volcanic eruption, this fire coming down from heaven, was God's wrath. The Sibylline Oracles stated:

> Fire shall come flashing forth in the broad heaven, And many cities burn and men destroy, And much black ashes shall fill the great sky, And small drops like red earth shall fall from heaven, Then **know the anger of the God of heaven**[155]

(For more information about this event read "The Destruction of Pompeii—God's Revenge?" by Hershel Shanks.[156])

---

155 "Sibylline Oracles, Book IV." n.d. Holy, Holy, Holy. Accessed December 10, 2022. https://trisagionseraph.tripod.com/Texts/Sibyl4.html.

156 Shanks, Hershel. 2022. "The Destruction of Pompeii—God's Revenge?" Biblical Archaeology Society. https://www.biblicalarchaeology.org/daily/ancient-cultures/ancient-near-eastern-world/the-destruction-of-pompeii-gods-revenge/.

Summary

Faithless Jerusalem and unbelieving Rome were worthy of the titles "Gog and Magog." When Satan was released, he used their bond to deceive the world into blaming the fire of Rome on the Christians. The unbelieving Jews, acting like Haman, conspired with Nero to exterminate the Christians; this was Satan deceiving the Roman empire to bring a terrible, empire-wide persecution against the saints. However, in the end, Rome turned against Jerusalem and burned her down. Meanwhile, God destroyed Rome in the fires of Vesuvius. As the fires destroyed the pagan temples of Rome, its worshipers believed their deities no longer existed.

While students of the Bible continue to question the identities of these characters and events, this scenario proves that Bible prophecy was fulfilled on time.

Suppose Jesus did return in the first century. Such a belief raises other questions and concerns. If Jesus has already returned, what are Christians still doing here? How do sin and death still exist? The next two chapters will bring satisfactory answers.

Chapter 16
No More Death

As illustrated in Chapter 8, "The Millennium's Approaching End," John prophesied that soon after he wrote the book of Revelation there would be no more death or pain (Revelation 21:1-4). Believers have misapplied the promise of no more death and pain to apply to earth, but this promise referred to the new heaven. Heaven had just become accessible at the resurrection when Hades was defeated.

Two Types of Death

While the word "death" in the Bible primarily describes the death of our earthly bodies, it sometimes describes the experience of Hades in the afterlife. In contrast, the Bible never describes someone in heaven as "dead" (Hebrews 10:12-13; 11:5).

Before the resurrection, the saints slept in Sheol or Hades and did not have the opportunity to enter heaven (see Chapter 6 The First Century Resurrection). However, after the resurrection, when the coming age had arrived, Christians inherited eternal life and were promised to never die. In the following passage notice that eternal life was given in the age to come:

> Mark 10:29-31 Jesus said, "Truly, I say to you, there is no one who has left house or brothers or sisters or mother or father or children or lands, for my sake and for the gospel, 30 who will not receive a hundredfold now in this time,

> houses and brothers and sisters and mothers and children and lands, with persecutions, **and in the age to come eternal life**.

In the passage below, a Christian is promised to "never die" after the resurrection. Although Christians have continued to die ever since the resurrection, they immediately go to heaven and are not considered "dead." Jesus promised:

> John 11:25-27 (BLB) the one believing in Me, even if he should die, he will live. And everyone living and believing in Me shall never die, to the age. Do you believe this?"

Though Abraham, Isaac, and Jacob are considered "dead" from an earthly perspective, they are considered "living" from heaven's perspective after the resurrection.

> Luke 20:37-38 (ESV) But that the dead are raised, even Moses showed, in the passage about the bush, where he calls the Lord the God of Abraham and the God of Isaac and the God of Jacob. 38 **Now he is not God of the dead, but of the living**...

Therefore, when the Bible describes "death" it can more specifically mean "*to be in Hades*."

No More Death Means No More Hades

Death was defeated when believers stopped going to Hades and began going to heaven where they are considered *living*.

A few verses after Hades was thrown into the lake of fire, John rejoiced that death was no more (Revelation 21:1-4).

> Revelation 20:14 Then Death and **Hades** were thrown into the lake of fire. This is the second death, the lake of fire.

> Revelation 21:4 (ESV) He will wipe away every tear from their eyes, **and death shall be no more**, neither shall there be mourning, nor crying, nor pain anymore, **for the former things have passed away**.

No Death or Pain in Heaven

Heaven had just become available to the saints at the resurrection at the Great White Throne Judgment (Hebrews 11:16,40; 13:14). Such a universe-changing reality would certainly have been in focus in the following chapter of Revelation, chapter 21.

The interpretation that no more pain describes heaven is confirmed when Revelation 21:4-7 is compared to Revelation 17:14-17. In chapter 17, the saints who came out of the Great Tribulation were said to "hunger no more, neither thirst anymore," have "every tear" wiped from their eyes, and drink from "springs of living water." It should be emphasized that these saints are "before the throne of God," clarifying that heaven is the realm where they experience these blessings.

> Revelation 17:14-17 (ESV) I said to him, "Sir, you know." And he said to me, "These are the ones coming out of the great tribulation. They have washed their robes and made them white in the blood of the Lamb. 15 "Therefore **they are before the throne of God**, and serve him day and night **in his temple**; and he who sits on the throne will shelter them **with his presence**. 16 They shall hunger no more, neither thirst anymore; the sun shall not strike them, nor any

> scorching heat. 17 For the Lamb in the midst of the throne will be their shepherd, and he will guide them to springs of living water, and God will wipe away every tear from their eyes."

The same terms are used in Revelation 21: "To the thirsty I will give from the spring of the water of life" (Revelation 21:6 [ESV]), and "He will wipe away every tear from their eyes" (Revelation 21:4 [ESV]). Both passages describe the wonderful new reality of heaven that had just opened up.

Earthly Death Continues

Earthly death was never promised to cease. Instead, the angel of Revelation pronounced a blessing on those who would die on earth from then on.

> Revelation 14:13 (ESV) And I heard a voice from heaven saying, "Write this: Blessed are the dead who die in the Lord from now on." "Blessed indeed," says the Spirit, "that they may rest from their labors, for their deeds follow them!"

Revelation further hints that pain continues to exist on earth because nations continue to receive healing from the tree of life (Revelation 22:1-2), and the wicked continue to exist outside the city (Revelation 21:6-8,27; 22:14-16).

One may also infer that sin exists in the age that was coming, or the *exclusive* New Covenant age, because Jesus said in the age that was to come, someone who spoke a word against the Holy Spirit would not be forgiven. If this age had no sin, how could someone speak a word against the Holy Spirit?

> Matthew 12:32 (JST) And whoever speaks a word against the Son of man, it shall be remitted to him; but whoever speaks against the Holy Spirit, it shall not be let go to him, neither in this time [age], nor that about to be.

New Heavens and Earth in Isaiah

Isaiah provides additional information on the new heavens and earth of Revelation and makes it clear that death and sin will continue to exist on earth.

Hostile Nations Perish

In the following passages, one can see Isaiah 60:19-20 describes the same reality as Revelation 21:23-27. Still, Isaiah adds that "the nation and kingdom that will not serve you shall perish," indicating that even in this age, death will exist on earth.

> Isaiah 60:19-20 (ESV) The sun shall be no more your light by day, nor for brightness shall the moon give you light; but the Lord will be your everlasting light, and your God will be your glory. 20 Your sun shall no more go down, nor your moon withdraw itself; for the Lord will be your everlasting light, and your days of mourning shall be ended.

> Isaiah 60:10-12 (ESV) Foreigners shall build up your walls, and their kings shall minister to you; for in my wrath I struck you, but in my favor I have had mercy on you. 11 Your gates shall be open continually; day and night they shall not be shut, that people may bring to you the wealth of the nations, with their kings led in procession. 12 **For the nation and kingdom that will not serve you shall perish; those nations shall be utterly laid waste.**

> Revelation 21:23-27 (NIV) The city does not need the sun or the moon to shine on it, for the glory of God gives it light, and the Lamb is its lamp. 24 The nations will walk by its light, and the kings of the earth will bring their splendor into it. 25 On no day will its gates ever be shut, for there will be no night there. 26 The glory and honor of the nations will be brought into it. 27 Nothing impure will ever enter it, nor will anyone who does what is shameful or deceitful, but only those whose names are written in the Lamb's book of life.

Sinners Die a Hundred Years Old

In another passage, Isaiah explicitly says that in the new heavens and earth, sinners will die at a hundred years old. He specifically mentions that it is the "sinner" who dies. He would not make such a distinction if he meant "no one will die."

> Isaiah 65:17-22 (ESV) "For behold, I create new heavens and a new earth, and the former things shall not be remembered or come into mind. 18 But be glad and rejoice forever in that which I create; for behold, I create Jerusalem to be a joy, and her people to be a gladness. 19 I will rejoice in Jerusalem and be glad in my people; no more shall be heard in it the sound of weeping and the cry of distress. 20 No more shall there be in it an infant who lives but a few days, or an old man who does not fill out his days, **for the young man shall die a hundred years old, and the sinner a hundred years old shall be accursed**. 21 They shall build houses and inhabit them; they shall plant vineyards and eat their fruit. 22 They shall not build and another inhabit; they shall not plant and another eat; **for**

> **like the days of a tree shall the days of my people be**, and my chosen shall long enjoy the work of their hands.

The above passage is a depiction of the kingdom of heaven as it exists on earth and in heaven. The sinner dies on earth and never enters heaven. Although he lived to be one hundred years old, he is young when compared to the saint who lives forever. The saint is promised to have the lifespan of a tree: "for like the days of a tree shall the days of my people be." To a Jewish reader in Isaiah's time, such an analogy meant that the saint would live forever. Scientists today debate if trees die of old age since some have existed for thousands of years.[157] Josephus even said,

> There is also there shewed, at the distance of six furlongs from the city, a very large turpentine tree; and the report goes that this tree has continued ever since the creation of the world.[158]

The saint begins his existence on earth and continues to live forever in heaven when his earthly body passes.

Isaiah and John both prophesy about the same new heavens and new earth. They use identical language, and Isaiah promises that the new heavens and earth will last forever.

In each passage:

- God creates a new heavens and earth (Isaiah 65:17; Revelation 21:1),

---

[157] Pomeroy, Ross. 2014. "Do Trees Die of Old Age?" RealClearScience. https://www.realclearscience.com/blog/2014/11/do_trees_die_of_old_age.html.

[158] Josephus, War, 4.9.7, http://penelope.uchicago.edu/josephus/war-4.html.

- the former things are not remembered (Isaiah 65:19; Revelation 21:4),
- the sound of weeping is heard no more (Isaiah 65:19; Revelation 21:4),
- God rejoices in his people Jerusalem (Isaiah 65:18-19; Revelation 21:2-3).

Isaiah also promises that the new heavens and earth will last forever.

> Isaiah 65:18 (ESV) But be glad and rejoice **forever** in that which I create

> Isaiah 66:22-23 (ESV) For **as the new heavens and the new earth that I make shall remain before me**, says the Lord, so shall your offspring and your name remain. 23 From new moon to new moon, and from Sabbath to Sabbath, all flesh shall come to worship before me, declares the Lord.

Something that lasts forever is not later replaced. Therefore, both prophecies about the new heavens and earth must describe the one and same establishment.

Justice is Needed

Jesus promised to rule forever, administering justice. There is no need for justice where there is no injustice, so sin must exist on earth to some degree. In Isaiah's idea of the new heavens and earth, death and evil are a regular part.

> Isaiah 9:7 (ESV) Of the increase of his government and of peace there will be no end, on the throne of David and over his kingdom, to establish it and to uphold it with justice

and with righteousness from this time forth and forevermore. The zeal of the Lord of hosts will do this.

Metaphorical Language

While the cosmic language used in Isaiah and Revelation can confuse the 21st century reader, it should be noted that both Isaiah and Revelation use metaphorical language which cannot be taken literally. "No more night" (Isaiah 60:19-20; Revelation 21:23-25), if taken literally, is contradicted when Isaiah says day and night will exist in the new heavens and new earth.

> Isaiah 60:19-20 (NIV) **The sun will no more be your light by day, nor will the brightness of the moon shine on you**, for **the Lord will be your everlasting light**, and your God will be your glory. 20 **Your sun will never set again**, and **your moon will wane no more**; the Lord will be your everlasting light, and your days of sorrow will end.

> Isaiah 60:11 (NIV) Your gates will always stand open, they will never be shut, **day or night**, so that people may bring you the wealth of the nations— their kings led in triumphal procession.

> Isaiah 66:23 (NIV) **From one New Moon to another** and **from one Sabbath to another**, all mankind will come and bow down before me," says the Lord.

Summary

Revelation and Isaiah never promise an end to death, sin, and pain on the new earth.

- Justice will always be needed on earth (Isaiah 9:7).
- The sinner will die a hundred years old (Isaiah 65:20).

- Nations that do not serve God's kingdom will perish (Isaiah 60:12).
- Revelation pronounces a blessing on those who die from that time onward (Revelation 14:13).

The promise of no more death, pain, and sin describes the new heaven that had just opened up to those in Christ at the resurrection (Revelation 17:14-17; 20:14; 21:4).

For Christians living today, eternal life begins the moment they believe (Mark 10:29-31). Although their earthly bodies will die, scripturally, they are not considered "dead" (Luke 20:37-38; John 11:25-26) because they go to heaven, not Sheol.

Although Revelation 21 primarily describes heaven, it has an earthly component. Just as the New Jerusalem comes out of heaven, God's kingdom descends upon this earth (Revelation 21:2-3). It continually grows here, bringing God's will, justice, peace, righteousness, and joy (Romans 14:17).

Chapter 17
What Now?

A natural question that Christians sometimes ask after hearing that Christ returned is "If Jesus has already returned, why am I still here? Do Christians have any purpose in being here?"

Of course! Preaching the gospel continues throughout the new age.

> Daniel 12:2-3 (ESV) And many of those who sleep in the dust of the earth shall awake, some to everlasting life, and some to shame and everlasting contempt. 3 And those who are wise shall shine like the brightness of the sky above; **and those who turn many to righteousness, like the stars forever and ever**.

Truthfully, Christians should be very hopeful!

Is This Ship Sinking?

Suppose one lives in the last generation on earth, and Jesus is about to come in his future to destroy and remake the planet. In that case, why invest in the affairs of this world? Why polish brass on a sinking ship? One's top priority would be to save as many as possible and keep himself safe from the tribulation. As Paul says,

> 1 Corinthians 7:29-31 (ESV) This is what I mean, brothers: the appointed time has grown very short. From now on, let those who have wives live as though they had none, 30 and those who mourn as though they were not mourning, and those who rejoice as though they were not rejoicing, and

> those who buy as though they had no goods, 31 and those who deal with the world as though they had no dealings with it. For the present form of this world is passing away.

Why build libraries, schools, hospitals, and research centers when such efforts will be futile, and Christ intends to destroy the world in our lifetime?

One can imagine how such a perspective can hinder sincere ministry efforts. Ministries could be more effective if they were more engaged in building this world and not making failed predictions of the end.

A World Without End

Scripture promised this world would last forever. After Noah's flood, God even promised to never destroy everyone on the earth again.

> Genesis 8:21-22 (WEB) Yahweh smelled the pleasant aroma. Yahweh said in his heart, "I will not again curse the ground any more for man's sake because the imagination of man's heart is evil from his youth. **I will never again strike every living thing, as I have done**. While the earth remains, seed time and harvest, and cold and heat, and summer and winter, and day and night will not cease."

> Psalm 148:1-6 (WEB) Praise Yah! Praise Yahweh from the heavens! Praise him in the heights! Praise him, all his angels! Praise him, all his army! Praise him, sun and moon! Praise him, all you shining stars! Praise him, you heavens of heavens, you waters that are above the heavens. Let them praise Yahweh's name, for he commanded, and they

were created. **He has also established them forever and ever. He has made a decree which will not pass away.**

Psalm 78:69 (WEB) He built his sanctuary like the heights, **like the earth which he has established forever**.

Ecclesiastes 1:4 (WEB) One generation goes, and another generation comes; **but the earth remains forever**.

Ephesians 3:21 (WEB) to him be the glory in the assembly and in Christ Jesus **to all generations forever and ever**. Amen.

Psalm 104:5 (WEB) He laid the foundations **of the earth, that it should not be moved forever**.

Psalm 119:90 (WEB) Your faithfulness is to all generations. **You have established the earth, and it remains**.

Most Christians believe Peter promised an end to earth in 2 Peter 3:10-12. However, Peter uses "earth" (or in Greek "gē,") to refer to the land of Israel, which did burn with fire during the final siege of 70 AD. The "elements" or "stoicheia" do not refer to the periodic table of elements but to the "elements of religious training or the ceremonial precepts."[159] It referred to the Old Covenant temple system.

2 Peter 3:10-12 (WEB) But the day of the Lord will come as a thief in the night; in which the heavens will pass away with a great noise, and the **elements [stoicheia]** will be dissolved with fervent heat, and the **earth [gē]** and the works that are in it will be burned up.

---

[159] "Strong's Greek: 4747. στοιχεῖον (stoicheion) -- one of a row, hence a letter (of the alphabet), by ext. the elements (of knowledge)." n.d. Bible Hub. Accessed February 12, 2023. https://biblehub.com/greek/4747.htm.

The word "earth" or in Greek "gē"[160] also means "land," and the word is often used to describe specific regions: the "land of Judah" (Matthew 2:6), the "land of Israel" (Matthew 2:20-21), the "land of Zebulun" and the "land of Naphtali (Matthew 4:15), "the land" or localized region where Jesus preached (Matthew 9:26,31), "the land of Sodom and Gomorrah" (Matthew 10:15), and "the land of Sodom" (Matthew 11:24).

The word "elements" or in Greek "stoicheia" means:

> [4747 (stoixeíon) refers to "the rudiments with which mankind . . . were indoctrinated (before the time of Christ), i.e. the elements of religious training or the ceremonial precepts common alike to the worship of Jews and of Gentiles" (J. Thayer).[161]

Notice that "elements" (Greek word stoicheion) is always used in the sense of "elements of religious training" throughout the New Testament.

> Galatians 4:3 (WEB) So we also, when we were children, were held in bondage under the **elemental** principles of the world.

> Galatians 4:9-10 (WEB) But now that you have come to know God, or rather to be known by God, why do you turn back again to the weak and miserable **elemental** principles, to which you desire to be in bondage all over again? You observe days, months, seasons, and years.

---

160 "Strong's Greek: 1093. γῆ (gé) -- the earth, land." n.d. Bible Hub. Accessed December 9, 2022. https://biblehub.com/greek/1093.htm.

161 Strong's Greek, stoicheion, https://biblehub.com/greek/4747.htm.

> Colossians 2:8 (WEB) Be careful that you don't let anyone rob you through his philosophy and vain deceit, **after the tradition of men, after the elements of the world**, and not after Christ.

> Colossians 2:20-22 (WEB) If you died with Christ from the **elements** of the world, why, as though living in the world, do you subject yourselves to ordinances, "Don't handle, nor taste, nor touch" (all of which perish with use), **according to the precepts and doctrines of men?**

> Hebrews 5:12 (NIV) In fact, though by this time you ought to be teachers, you need someone to teach you the **elementary** truths of God's word all over again. You need milk, not solid food!

The Bible promises that the world will last forever, not end. However, the land of Israel and the Old Covenant temple system with its traditions of men would burn.

Since this world will be here forever, God's people have a purpose beyond saving the lost. They are to spread the kingdom of heaven on earth and improve the world for themselves and their children. In doing so, they win the world's respect and make the gospel more attractive.

The Kingdom Came with Christ

One may assume that if all prophecy was fulfilled in the first century, Christians have nothing left. However, Christ's return marked the arrival of the kingdom of heaven. It was a new beginning!

Mark 9:1 (ESV) And he said to them, "Truly, I say to you, there are some standing here **who will not taste death until they see the kingdom of God after it has come with power**."

Luke 21:31-32 (ESV) So also, when you see these things taking place, you know that the kingdom of God is near. 32 Truly, I say to you, this generation will not pass away until all has taken place.

Christ's return corresponded with the arrival of the kingdom of heaven. This is good news, indeed!

The Kingdom Grows

God's kingdom will never be conquered but will continually increase in this world, bringing peace, joy, justice, and righteousness (Isaiah 11:1-9).

Isaiah 9:7 (ESV) Of the increase of his government and of peace there will be no end, on the throne of David and over his kingdom, to establish it and to uphold it with justice and with righteousness from this time forth and forevermore. The zeal of the LORD of hosts will do this.

Daniel 2:32-35 (ESV) Then the iron [Rome], the clay [Roman Empire split into 10 provinces], the bronze [Greece], the silver [Persia], and the gold [Babylon], all together were broken in pieces, and became like the chaff of the summer threshing floors; and the wind carried them away, so that not a trace of them could be found. But the stone that struck the image [God's kingdom] became a great mountain and filled the whole earth.

Daniel 2:44 (ESV) And in the days of those kings the God of heaven will set up a kingdom that shall never be destroyed, nor shall the kingdom be left to another people. It shall break in pieces all these kingdoms and bring them to an end, and it shall stand forever

Hebrews 12:28 (ESV) Therefore let us be grateful for receiving a kingdom that cannot be shaken, and thus let us offer to God acceptable worship, with reverence and awe

Revelation 11:15 (ESV) Then the seventh angel blew his trumpet, and there were loud voices in heaven, saying, "The kingdom of the world has become the kingdom of our Lord and of his Christ, and he shall reign forever and ever."

Matthew 13:31-33 (ESV) He put another parable before them, saying, "The kingdom of heaven is like a grain of mustard seed that a man took and sowed in his field. 32 It is the smallest of all seeds, but when it has grown it is larger than all the garden plants and becomes a tree, so that the birds of the air come and make nests in its branches." 33 He told them another parable. "The kingdom of heaven is like leaven that a woman took and hid in three measures of flour, till it was all leavened."

Romans 14:17 (ESV) For the kingdom of God is not a matter of eating and drinking but of righteousness and peace and joy in the Holy Spirit.

Revelation 5:10 (ESV) And you have made them a kingdom and priests to our God, and they shall reign on the earth."

1 Peter 2:9 (WEB) But you [Christians] are a chosen race, a royal priesthood, a holy nation, a people for God's own possession, that you may proclaim the excellence of him who called you out of darkness into his marvelous light.

Isaiah 32:1 (ESV) Behold, a king will reign in righteousness, and princes will rule in justice.

Yeast spreading through dough? A mustard seed growing into the largest of garden plants? The stone growing into a mountain and filling the earth? Of the increase of his kingdom, there will be no end? Jesus planted the seed of his kingdom upon his arrival, and it continues to grow forever, filling the earth with justice, righteousness, peace, and joy.

The Kingdom is Invisible

Jesus says this kingdom is like the wind; one cannot see and point to a specific person, country, or army and say, "That is the kingdom!" However, it is the most significant force on earth.

Luke 17:20-21 (ESV) Being asked by the Pharisees when the kingdom of God would come, he answered them, "The kingdom of God is not coming with signs to be observed, nor will they say, 'Look, here it is!' or 'There!' for behold, the kingdom of God is in the midst of you."

John 3:3-8 (ESV) Jesus answered him, "Truly, truly, I say to you, unless one is born again he cannot see the kingdom of God." 4 Nicodemus said to him, "How can a man be born when he is old? Can he enter a second time into his mother's womb and be born?" 5 Jesus answered, "Truly, truly, I say to you, unless one is born of water and the Spirit, he cannot enter the kingdom of God. 6 That which is born of the flesh is flesh, and that which is born of the Spirit is spirit. 7 Do not marvel that I said to you, 'You must be born again.' 8 The wind blows where it wishes, and you hear its sound, but you do not know where it comes from or where it goes. So it is with everyone who is born of the Spirit."

John 18:36 (WEB) Jesus answered, “My Kingdom is not of this world. If my Kingdom were of this world, then my servants would fight, that I wouldn’t be delivered to the Jews. But now my Kingdom is not from here.”

Matthew 6:10 (ESV) Your kingdom come, your will be done, on earth as it is in heaven.

God carries out his will on earth through his kingdom.

Who Is in the Kingdom?

The poor (Matthew 5:3), those persecuted for righteousness sake (Matthew 5:10), the little children (Matthew 19:14), and those born of water and Spirit (John 3:5) inherit the kingdom of heaven.

Daniel 7:27 (ESV) And the kingdom and the dominion and the greatness of the kingdoms under the whole heaven shall be given to the people of the saints of the Most High; their kingdom shall be an everlasting kingdom, and all dominions shall serve and obey them.

Luke 12:32 (ESV) Fear not, little flock, for it is your Father's good pleasure to give you the kingdom.

Matthew 25:34 (ESV) Then the King will say to those on his right, 'Come, you who are blessed by my Father, inherit the kingdom prepared for you from the foundation of the world.

> Revelation 5:9-10 (ESV) for you were slain, and by your blood you ransomed people for God from every tribe and language and people and nation, 10 and you have made them a kingdom and priests to our God, and they shall reign on the earth.

Christians are members of this kingdom.

Blessings upon Kingdom Members

Is it better to live in the age that awaited the promises or the age that inherits them? In this age and forever, Christians inherit God's great blessings. While they still may face persecution, they are not without God's favor in this life and may ask him for anything.

God promises abundance and joy upon his people.

> Isaiah 60:5 (ESV) Then you shall see and be radiant; your heart shall thrill and exult, because the abundance of the sea shall be turned to you, the wealth of the nations shall come to you.

> Isaiah 61:6 (ESV) but you shall be called the priests of the Lord; they shall speak of you as the ministers of our God; you shall eat the wealth of the nations, and in their glory you shall boast.

God promises his people honor, peace, and deliverance from their enemies. If anyone attacks them, it will not be God's doing, and they will surrender.

> Isaiah 62:2 (ESV) The nations shall see your righteousness, and all the kings your glory, and you shall be called by a new name that the mouth of the Lord will give.

Isaiah 66:12 (ESV) For thus says the Lord: "Behold, I will extend peace to her like a river, and the glory of the nations like an overflowing stream; and you shall nurse, you shall be carried upon her hip, and bounced upon her knees."

Isaiah 54:13-17 (ESV) All your children shall be taught by the Lord, and great shall be the peace of your children. 14 In righteousness you shall be established; you shall be far from oppression, for you shall not fear; and from terror, for it shall not come near you. 15 If anyone stirs up strife, it is not from me; whoever stirs up strife with you shall fall because of you. 16 Behold, I have created the smith who blows the fire of coals and produces a weapon for its purpose. I have also created the ravager to destroy; 17 no weapon that is fashioned against you shall succeed, and you shall refute every tongue that rises against you in judgment. This is the heritage of the servants of the Lord and their vindication from me, declares the Lord."

God promises no more judgment, anger, curse, or wrath upon the saints.

Isaiah 54:9 (ESV) "This is like the days of Noah to me: as I swore that the waters of Noah should no more go over the earth, so I have sworn that I will not be angry with you, and will not rebuke you.

Isaiah 65:22 (ESV) They shall not build and another inhabit; they shall not plant and another eat; for like the days of a tree shall the days of my people be, and my chosen shall long enjoy the work of their hands.

Christianity will spread to the ends of the earth.

> Isaiah 9:7 (ESV) Of the increase of his government and of peace there will be no end, on the throne of David and over his kingdom, to establish it and to uphold it with justice and with righteousness from this time forth and forevermore. The zeal of the Lord of hosts will do this.

Nations that do not serve his kingdom will perish.

> Isaiah 60:12 (ESV) For the nation and kingdom that will not serve you shall perish; those nations shall be utterly laid waste.

The Lord will delight in his people and call them married (Isaiah 62). God will not rest until making Christianity the praise of the earth.

> Isaiah 62:7 (ESV) and give him no rest until he establishes Jerusalem and makes it a praise in the earth.

Believers are the New Jerusalem (Galatians 4:26), so these promises apply to them.

United in Christ

In chapter 11, Isaiah talks about animals living at peace with each other (Isaiah 11:6-9).

> Isaiah 11:6,10 (ESV) The wolf will live with the lamb... 10 In that day the root of Jesse, who shall stand as a signal for the peoples—of him shall the nations inquire, and his resting place shall be glorious.

However, when taken in context of Isaiah 11, the verse about the wolf and lamb is meant to be understood metaphorically. Paul quotes Isaiah chapter 11 in Romans 15:12, interpreting it to mean that the Christian Gentile (wolf) and the Christian Jew (lamb) should welcome each other and that they should be united and at peace with each other through their shared faith.

> Romans 15:7-12 (ESV) **Therefore welcome one another as Christ has welcomed you**, for the glory of God. 8 For I tell you that Christ became a servant to the circumcised to show God's truthfulness, in order to confirm the promises given to the patriarchs, 9 and in order that the Gentiles might glorify God for his mercy. As it is written, "Therefore I will praise you among the Gentiles, and sing to your name." 10 And again it is said, "Rejoice, O Gentiles, with his people." 11 And again, "Praise the Lord, all you Gentiles, and let all the peoples extol him." 12 **And again Isaiah says, "The root of Jesse will come, even he who arises to rule the Gentiles; in him will the Gentiles hope."**

Although people from each nation differ in many aspects, they find unity and peace through their shared faith in Christ.

The Improving World

God's kingdom is continually improving this world. Early church father Eusebius, writing around 314 AD, said that ever since Christ's birth, the world has experienced unprecedented peace.

> For unexampled peace has filled all nations from the time of His coming: no longer do states war with states as before, nor nations contend with nations, nor is human life as of old in a state of constant disturbance; Athenians do not attack (458) Lacedaemonians, Syrians Phoenicians, Arabians the inhabitants of Palestine, nor the Egyptians their neighbours. All have been united from that time by God's help, and it is true that there has been "abundance of

peace" among the nations from that day to this, according to the prophecy...

> Isaiah, too, agrees with this when he says, "And they shall beat their swords into ploughshares, and their lances into pruning-hooks; nation shall not take up sword against nation, and they shall not learn war any more." You will find Micah in agreement with this, and many other prophets. And if you note, as I said, the dates, you will be able to appreciate that from the time of Augustus, and of the Epiphany of our Saviour that shone forth in his day, during the period of the Roman Empire the old dissensions and varieties of national government have ceased, and thus from that date the peace of the prophecy began. Just as it then began, a day will come when the prophecy will be fulfilled in all its fullness, when, as the apostle says, "the fullness of the Gentiles shall come in."[162]

Looking at average statistics around the world, it is clear the world is much better than it was fifty years ago, two hundred years ago, and two thousand years ago. This improvement is like the stock market; in the long run, it always climbs, but sometimes it has scary dips. J. D. King shares some encouraging findings in his article "Is The World Getting Worse?" He writes:

> Dr. Steven Pinker, Pulitzer prize-winning author and Harvard psychology professor noted that "Today we may be living in the most peaceful era in our species' existence."[1] Prior to the Second World War, nations were continually in bloody conflict. Many Western European nations initiated

---

162 Eusebius, Demonstratio Evangelica, 9.17.187-188, http://www.intratext.com/IXT/ENG0882/_P3T.HTM.

war every two to three years. However, since the peak of the Cold War in the 1980s, civil wars, genocides, and terrorist attacks—have significantly diminished throughout the world.

...

"England, Canada, and most other industrialized countries have also seen their homicide rates fall in the past decade. Among the 88 countries with reliable data, 67 have seen a decline in the past 15 years...Rates of rape or sexual assault and of violence against intimate partners have been sinking for decades, and are now a quarter or less of their peaks in the past."[3]

...

Archeologists and anthropologists have surmised that over 15% of society died violently in previous centuries. More recently this number has dropped down to 3%. In the Twenty-First Century less than 1% have died a violent or war-related death.[4]

...

Summarizing his findings, Pinker writes that,

"The world is not falling apart. The kinds of violence to which most people are vulnerable—homicide, rape, battering, child abuse—have been in steady decline in most of the world. Autocracy is giving way to democracy. Wars between states—by far the most destructive of all conflicts—are all but obsolete. The increase in the number and deadliness of civil wars since 2010 is circumscribed, puny in comparison with the decline that preceded it, and unlikely to escalate."[163]

J. D. King's article shows how poverty is falling worldwide, health and life expectancies are increasing everywhere, and Christianity is multiplying in almost every country.

Our World in Data[164] has been collecting statistics on all measurements of human progress: death, life expectancy, crime, wealth, health, peace, and other states of progress. When browsing their charts, one finds that with few exceptions almost every part of the world has been improving.

Although there will continue to be wars, crime, or other issues to combat, God has made significant progress. Slavery was outlawed worldwide over one and a half centuries ago; that is a monumental victory. Christianity has grown from twelve disciples to over two billion Christians,[165] showing the significant expansion of God's kingdom.

Overwhelming Blessings

While the growing kingdom provides more hope and purpose here, Christ's arrival brings many other wonderful benefits.

---

163 King, J. D. 2015. "Is The World Getting Worse?" Charisma Magazine. https://charismamag.com/spriritled-living/woman/is-the-world-getting-worse/.

164 Roser, Max. n.d. "About." Our World in Data. Accessed December 14, 2022. https://ourworldindata.org/about.

165 eglitis-media. n.d. "Christianity - Worldwide distribution." Worlddata.info. Accessed December 9, 2022. https://www.worlddata.info/religions/christianity.php.

- Christians now go to heaven, not Hades
- The Old Covenant has fully ended
- One can finally understand the Bible and answer the skeptics

Each of these will be explained more in the following sections.

Christians in Heaven, Not Hades

With the defeat of Sheol/Hades (Revelation 20:14), the believer goes immediately to heaven to enjoy eternal bliss in the presence of God. Their good deeds follow (Revelation 14:13). Gone is the wait for resurrection from the underworld of Sheol. It is comforting to know our Christian loved ones who have passed on are now with God in heaven looking down on us.

The Old Covenant Ended

The Mosaic law officially ended when all prophecy was accomplished; the old heaven and earth passed away (Luke 21:22,31-33; Revelation 21:1).

> Matthew 5:18 (ESV) For truly, I say to you, until heaven and earth pass away, not an iota, not a dot, will pass from the Law until all is accomplished.

The Romans burned down the temple. Just as Jesus predicted, not one stone was left upon another (Matthew 14:2). With the ancestral records of the Levites destroyed, authentic practice of the Mosaic law became impossible. The Old Covenant had officially ended.

Even though the disciples died to the law in the body of Christ and were not obligated to keep it (Romans 7:2-4; Galatians 3:24-25), the Jewish Christians continued to practice it for the sake of helping unbelieving Jews come to the gospel (1 Corinthians 9:19-23).

When the Mosaic law officially ended, it no longer aided their ministries. Today, God does not require the keeping of the Mosaic law for any reason; instead, Christians live by the Spirit. God writes his will on their hearts. Jeremiah describes the terms of this New Covenant.

> Jeremiah 31:31-34 (ESV) "Behold, the days are coming, declares the Lord, when I will make a new covenant with the house of Israel and the house of Judah, 32 not like the covenant that I made with their fathers on the day when I took them by the hand to bring them out of the land of Egypt, my covenant that they broke, though I was their husband, declares the Lord. 33 For this is the covenant that I will make with the house of Israel after those days, declares the Lord: I will put my law within them, and I will write it on their hearts. And I will be their God, and they shall be my people. 34 And no longer shall each one teach his neighbor and each his brother, saying, 'Know the Lord,' for they shall all know me, from the least of them to the greatest, declares the Lord. For I will forgive their iniquity, and I will remember their sin no more."

In this New Covenant, God is the one who changes hearts from the inside out and causes his people to walk in love.

> Philippians 2:13 (ISV) For it is God who is producing in you both the desire and the ability to do what pleases him.

> Romans 2:14-15 (ESV) For when Gentiles, who do not have the law, by nature do what the law requires, they are a law to themselves, even though they do not have the law. 15 They show that the work of the law is written on their hearts, while their conscience also bears witness, and their conflicting thoughts accuse or even excuse them

> Ezekiel 36:27 (ESV) And I will put my Spirit within you, and cause you to walk in my statutes and be careful to obey my rules.

If someone has the Spirit of God, the Spirit produces the desire and ability to live godly lives, even without the Mosaic law. And when Christians fail, they have his promise of unlimited grace and forgiveness to pick them up. Jesus paid the total price for our sins at the cross so that when we trust in him we can stand as righteous in God's presence (Romans 3:21-25).

> Romans 3:21-25 (ESV) But now the righteousness of God has been manifested apart from the law, although the Law and the Prophets bear witness to it— 22 the righteousness of God through faith in Jesus Christ for all who believe. For there is no distinction: 23 for all have sinned and fall short of the glory of God, 24 and are justified by his grace as a gift, through the redemption that is in Christ Jesus, 25 whom God put forward as a propitiation by his blood, to be received by faith.

Therefore, Christians have peace with God for all eternity and can feel grateful in their hearts for his unmerited favor!

> Romans 5:1-2 (ESV) Therefore, since we have been justified by faith, we have peace with God through our Lord Jesus

> Christ. 2 Through him we have also obtained access by faith into this grace in which we stand

God's grace and love make us grateful and transform us to love God and others more.

> Jeremiah 31:34 (ESV) For I will forgive their iniquity, and I will remember their sin no more.

> Luke 7:47 (ESV) Therefore I tell you, her sins, which are many, are forgiven—for she loved much. But he who is forgiven little, loves little.

> Titus 2:11-12 (NIV) For the grace of God has appeared that offers salvation to all people. It teaches us to say "No" to ungodliness and worldly passions, and to live self-controlled, upright and godly lives in this present age

> Romans 5:20-21 (ESV) Now the law came in to increase the trespass, but where sin increased, grace abounded all the more, so that, as sin reigned in death, grace also might reign through righteousness leading to eternal life through Jesus Christ our Lord.

The believer can always count on God's forgiveness in their life and on the work of the Spirit to change their heart.

Understanding the Bible

Those who believe Christ did not return on time struggle with many unanswered questions when reading the Bible. The competing beliefs undermine their faith, usually at a subconscious level. Now that it can be shown that Christ came on time, readers can hope to understand their Bible confidently. An on-time return unifies the scriptures, Old and

New Testament prophecies, makes sense of otherwise cryptic passages, gives confidence, and answers skeptics who claim Jesus was a false prophet.

The End of the End

The fear of the end times has crippled ministries, but Christ's on-time return will give confidence, purpose, and hope. The scriptures can be explained without gymnastics. Answers can be given to the Christian skeptics. Pessimism is replaced with hope.

Christ returned on time and that has wonderful implications for us today.

So much remains to be discovered, and researchers should study humbly, ready to correct their assumptions as they gain new information.

Let us open our Bibles, preferably one of the literal Greek and Hebrew translations, and keep asking questions. Instead of trusting in man's opinion, may we let scripture interpret scripture, and rely on the daily guidance of the Holy Spirit to lead us into all truth.

> Matthew 7:7 (ESV) Ask, and it will be given to you; seek, and you will find; knock, and it will be opened to you.

References

Alexandria, Eutychius o. 2014. The Annals. Translated by Roger Pearse. https://www.roger-pearse.com/weblog/eutychius-annals-my-posts-containing-the-translation/.

Anthony, Richard. n.d. "The Mark Of The Beast." ecclesia.org. Accessed December 10, 2022. http://www.ecclesia.org/truth/beast.html.

Apollodorus. 1921. Apollodorus, The Library. Translated by James G. Frazer. Loeb Classical Library ed. 2 vols. Cambridge, MA: Harvard University Press. http://www.perseus.tufts.edu/hopper/text?doc=Perseus:text:1999.01.0022:text=Library.

"Babylonian Talmud: Tractate Gittin." n.d. Chabad.org. Accessed December 10, 2022. https://www.chabad.org/media/pdf/323/YIxQ3233957.pdf.

BBC. 2020. "Hundreds of billions of locusts swarm in East Africa." BBC. https://www.bbc.com/news/in-pictures-51618188.

Beckwith, Isbon T. 2001. The Apocalypse of John. N.p.: Wipf & Stock Publishers.

Berean Bible Church. n.d. "THE OLIVET DISCOURSE CANNOT BE DIVIDED Chart." Berean Bible Church. Accessed December 9, 2022. https://www.bereanbiblechurch.org/transcripts/mark/13_32-37_chart.htm.

Brother A-aron. 2020. "Partial-Preterism! Approach to the Book of Revelation: Interview with Bruce Gore." YouTube. https://www.youtube.com/watch?v=aRJluO6AVIw.

Bullinger, Ethelbert W. 1902. The Rich Man and Lazarus: An Intermediate State? https://www.afterlife.co.nz/wp-content/uploads/2009/07/eb-rml1.pdf.

Caesarea, Andrew o. 2017. Commentary on the Apocalypse. Translated by Eugenia S. Constantinou. N.p.: Catholic University of America Press. https://preteristarchives.org/andreas-of-caesarea/.

Chilton, David. 1987. The Days of Vengeance: An Exposition of the Book of Revelation. N.p.: Dominion Press. https://www.reconstructionistradio.com/audiobook/the-days-of-vengeance/chapter-3-leviathan-and-behemoth-9/.

Cohen, Abraham. 1949. Everyman's Talmud with an introduction. New American ed. New York, NY: E.P. Dutton.

Constitutional Rights Foundation. n.d. "Constitutional Rights Foundation." Constitutional Rights Foundation. Accessed January 6, 2023. https://www.crf-usa.org/bill-of-rights-in-action/bria-13-4-b-religious-tolerance-and-persecution-in-the-roman-empire.

Cruickshank, Robert. 2021. "The Millennium: Significance of the Thousand Year Symbol (Rev 20:1-10)." YouTube. https://www.youtube.com/watch?v=wR9GWpSGyBU.

Cruickshank, Robert. 2022. "The First Resurrection (Rev. 20:4-5) - Bob Cruickshank Jr (2022 Conference)." YouTube. https://youtu.be/46hrjwTbHMc?t=655.

Cruickshank, Robert. 2022. "The Binding of Satan in the Gospels - Bob Cruickshank Jr (2022 Conference)." YouTube. https://www.youtube.com/watch?v=qSGjNP-S2n0.

Cruickshank, Robert. 2022. "Guest Article: Revelation, the Mark of the Beast- Part 1- By Robert ..." Preterist Research Institute. https://bibleprophecy.com/articles/2022/06/25/guest-article-revelation-the-mark-of-the-beast-part-1-by-robert-cruickshank/.

Dein, Simon. 2020. "Covid-19 and the Apocalypse: Religious and Secular Perspectives." NCBI. https://www.ncbi.nlm.nih.gov/pmc/articles/PMC7598223/.

DeMar, Gary. 2008. Why the End of the World is Not in Your Future, Identifying the Gog-Magog Alliance. Powder Springs, Georgia: American Vision Press.

DeMar, Gary. 2016. The Gog and Magog End-Time Alliance, Israel, Russia, and Syria in Bible Prophecy. Powder Springs, Georgia: American Vision Press.

Denton, Tony E. 2008. "What Will We Do With The Greek Term Mello?" A Site For The Lord | Bible Studies And Books.

http://asiteforthelord.com/wp-content/uploads/2017/09/MelloByTheScholars1.pdf.
Diamant, Jeff. 2022. "About four-in-ten U.S. adults believe humanity is 'living in the end times.'" Pew Research Center. https://www.pewresearch.org/fact-tank/2022/12/08/about-four-in-ten-u-s-adults-believe-humanity-is-living-in-the-end-times/.
Dimuro, Gina. 2018. "39 Agonizing Photos Of Pompeii's Bodies Frozen In Time." All That's Interesting. https://allthatsinteresting.com/bodies-of-pompeii.
Dio, Cassius. 1914. Roman History. Translated by Earnest Cary. Loeb Classical Library ed. 9 vols. N.p.: Harvard University Press. https://penelope.uchicago.edu/Thayer/E/Roman/Texts/Cassius_Dio/home.html.
Dunson, Ben C., Guest Contributor, and John Piper. 2021. "Where Do Christians Go When They Die?" Desiring God. https://www.desiringgod.org/articles/where-do-christians-go-when-they-die.
Eberle, Harold R., and Martin Trench. 2021. Victorious Eschatology: A Partial Preterist View. Kindle ed. Yakima, Washington: Worldcast Ministries & Publishing.
Eberle, Herald. 2011. "Victorious Eschatology - Part I." YouTube. https://www.youtube.com/watch?v=J5xDdkzlmWc.
Edgecombe, Daniel. 2020. "Echoes of the Baal Cycle in Scripture." Living Faith. https://living-faith.org/2020/01/17/echoes-of-the-baal-cycle-in-scripture/.
eglitis-media. n.d. "Christianity - Worldwide distribution." Worlddata.info. Accessed December 9, 2022. https://www.worlddata.info/religions/christianity.php.
Enns, Pete, and Christopher M. Hays. 2016. "When is Jesus Coming Back? Well, The Answer May Shock You." The Bible For Normal People. https://thebiblefornormalpeople.com/on-why-jesus-hasnt-come-back-yet/.
Evidence Unseen. n.d. "(Mt. 24:34) Did Jesus make a false prediction about his second coming?" Evidence Unseen. Accessed December 9, 2022. https://

www.evidenceunseen.com/bible-difficulties-2/nt-difficulties/matthew/mt-2434-did-jesus-make-a-false-prediction-about-his-second-coming/.

Geisler, Norman L. n.d. "A Review of Hank Hanegraaff's The Apocalypse Code – NORMAN GEISLER." Norman Geisler. Accessed December 9, 2022. https://normangeisler.com/a-review-of-hanegraaff-apocalypse-code/.

Gentry, Kenneth L. 2010. Before Jerusalem Fell: Dating the Book of Revelation. N.p.: Victorious Hope Publishing.

Got Questions Ministries. 2022. "What happens after death?" GotQuestions.org. https://www.gotquestions.org/what-happens-after-death.html.

Got Questions Ministries. n.d. "What did Jesus mean when He said, "this generation will not pass"?" gotquestions.org. Accessed December 8, 2022. https://www.gotquestions.org/this-generation-not-pass.html.

Green, David A. 2002. "Preterism 101." Preterist Cosmos. http://www.preteristcosmos.com/preterism101.html.

Habermas, Gary R. 2016. "Near Death Experiences: Evidence for an Afterlife? - Apologetics." North American Mission Board. https://www.namb.net/apologetics/resource/near-death-experiences-evidence-for-an-afterlife/.

Ice, Thomas D. 2009. "An Interpretation of Matthew 24-25." Article Archives, no. 2 (May). https://digitalcommons.liberty.edu/cgi/viewcontent.cgi?article=1001&context=pretrib_arch.

Irenaeus. 1885. Against Heresies, Ante-Nicene Fathers. Edited by James Donaldson, A. C. Coxe., and Kevin Knight. Translated by Alexander Roberts and William Rambaut. Vol. 1. Buffalo, NY: Christian Literature Publishing Co. https://www.newadvent.org/fathers/0103.htm.

Jones, Brian, and Robert Milns. 2002. Suetonius: The Flavian Emperors, A Historical Commentary. London: Bristol Classic Press.

Jordan, James B. 1995. Esther in the Midst of Covenant History. Niceville on the Bayou of the Bog, Florida: Biblical Horizons.

Josephus, Flavius, Samuel Burder, and William Whiston. 2015. The Genuine Works of Flavius Josephus, the Jewish Historian: Containing Twenty Books of the Jewish Antiquities, Seven Books of the Jewish War, and the Life of Josephus. N.p.: Creative Media Partners, LLC. http://penelope.uchicago.edu/josephus/index.html.

King, J. D. 2015. "Is The World Getting Worse?" Charisma Magazine. https://charismamag.com/spriritled-living/woman/is-the-world-getting-worse/.

Kirby, Peter. n.d. "Gospel of Nicodemus: The Descent of Christ into Hell (ANF text)." Early Christian Writings. Accessed December 9, 2022. http://www.earlychristianwritings.com/text/gospelnicodemus-roberts2.html.

Lewis, Clive S. 1960. The World's Last Night, and Other Essays. N.p.: Harcourt, Brace. https://archive.org/details/worldslastnighta012859mbp/page/n109/mode/2up.

"List of cities claimed to be built on seven hills." n.d. Wikipedia. Accessed December 10, 2022. https://en.wikipedia.org/wiki/List_of_cities_claimed_to_be_built_on_seven_hills.

Long, Jeffrey. 2014. "Near-Death Experiences Evidence for Their Reality." NCBI. https://www.ncbi.nlm.nih.gov/pmc/articles/PMC6172100/.

Lucey, Candice. 2021. "Why Was the Messiah Expected to Free Israel from Rome?" Christianity. https://www.christianity.com/wiki/jesus-christ/why-was-the-messiah-expected-to-free-israel-from-rome.html.

"Luke 12:36 Greek Text Analysis." n.d. Bible Hub. Accessed January 10, 2023. https://biblehub.com/text/luke/12-36.htm.

Maarschalk, Adam. 2017. "Did All of the Judean Christians Flee to Pella?" Adam Maarschalk. https://adammaarschalk.com/2017/01/24/did-all-of-the-judean-christians-flee-to-pella/.

Maarschalk, Adam. n.d. "Beast of Revelation – Pursuing Truth." Adam Maarschalk. Accessed December 31, 2022. https://adammaarschalk.com/beast-of-revelation/.

"Matthew 16:27 Greek Text Analysis." n.d. Bible Hub. Accessed December 30, 2022. https://biblehub.com/text/matthew/16-27.htm.

"Matthew 24:30 Greek Text Analysis." n.d. Bible Hub. Accessed December 9, 2022. https://biblehub.com/text/matthew/24-30.htm.

"Matthew 24:34 Greek Text Analysis." n.d. Bible Hub. Accessed January 9, 2023. https://biblehub.com/text/matthew/24-34.htm.

"Matthew 24:34 Greek Text Analysis." n.d. Bible Hub. Accessed January 25, 2023. https://biblehub.com/text/matthew/24-34.htm.

McKenzie, Duncan W. 2009. The Antichrist and the Second Coming: A Preterist Examination. Vol. II. N.p.: Xulon Press, Incorporated.

Morais, Daniel. 2017. "Matthew 24 Commentary: THAT Generation Shall Not Pass." Revelation Revolution Foundation. https://www.revelationrevolution.org/matthew-24-commentary-that-generation-shall-not-pass/.

Morais, Daniel. n.d. "The Flight and Return of the Christians, like the Exile and Return of the Jews from Babylon, is an Earthly Reflection of the Resurrection." Revelation Revolution Foundation. Accessed December 9, 2022. https://www.revelationrevolution.org/flight-return-christians-like-exile-return-jews-babylon-earthly-reflection-resurrection.

Morais, Daniel. n.d. "Revelation 11: A Preterist Commentary–Who are the Two Witnesses?" Revelation Revolution Foundation. Accessed December 10, 2022. https://www.revelationrevolution.org/revelation-11-a-preterist-commentary-who-are-the-two-witnesses/.

Morais, Daniel. n.d. "Revelation 13: A Preterist Commentary." Revelation Revolution Foundation. Accessed December 10, 2022. https://www.revelationrevolution.org/revelation-13-a-preterist-commentary/.

Morais, Daniel. n.d. "Revelation 16: A Preterist Commentary." Revelation Revolution Foundation. Accessed December 10,

2022. https://www.revelationrevolution.org/revelation-16-a-preterist-commentary/.
Morais, Daniel. n.d. "Revelation 17: A Preterist Commentary." Revelation Revolution Foundation. Accessed December 10, 2022. https://www.revelationrevolution.org/revelation-17-a-preterist-commentary/.
Morais, Daniel. n.d. "Revelation 9: A Preterist Commentary–Who is Apollyon?" Revelation Revolution Foundation. Accessed December 10, 2022. https://www.revelationrevolution.org/revelation-9-a-preterist-commentary-who-is-apollyon/.
Pamphilii of Caesarea, Eusebius. 1920. Demonstratio Evangelica of Eusebius of Caesarea, Translations of Christian Literature, Series 1, Greek Texts. Edited by W. J. Sparrow-Simpson and W. K. Lowther Clarke. Translated by William J. Ferrar. New York, NY: The Macmillan Company. http://www.intratext.com/X/ENG0882.HTM.
Pamphili of Caesarea, Eusebius. n.d. Church History. Translated by Nicene and Post-Nicene Fathers. Accessed Dec. 9, 2022. https://www.historytimeline.org/docs/eusebius/church_history/.
Paroschi, Wilson, and Engenheiro Coelho. 2013. "The Significance of a Comma: An Analysis of Luke 23:43." Ministry Magazine. https://www.ministrymagazine.org/archive/2013/06/the-significance-of-a-comma:-an-analysis-of-luke-23:43.
Pate, C. M., and Calvin B. Haines. 1995. Doomsday Delusions: What's Wrong with Predictions about the End of the World. N.p.: InterVasity Press.
"Philippians 1:23 Greek Text Analysis." n.d. Bible Hub. Accessed December 15, 2022. https://biblehub.com/text/philippians/1-23.htm.
Pomeroy, Ross. 2014. "Do Trees Die of Old Age?" RealClearScience. https://www.realclearscience.com/blog/2014/11/do_trees_die_of_old_age.html.
Pseudo. 2005. Hegesippus, translated from Latin into English. Translated by Wade Blocker. (This excerpt is taken from the

Latin edited by Vincent Ussani) ed. https://www.tertullian.org/fathers/hegesippus_00_eintro.htm.
"Revelation 11:8 Greek Text Analysis." n.d. Bible Hub. Accessed December 26, 2022. https://biblehub.com/text/revelation/11-8.htm.
Rosenauer, Joel. 2023. "Proceed With Caution." YouTube. https://www.youtube.com/watch?v=FFpzKVWvAVw.
Roser, Max. n.d. "About." Our World in Data. Accessed December 14, 2022. https://ourworldindata.org/about.
Schaff, Philip. 1996. History of the Christian church. N.p.: Hendrickson Publishers. https://ccel.org/ccel/schaff/hcc1/hcc1.i.VI.37.html.
"Seven hills of Rome." n.d. Wikipedia. Accessed December 10, 2022. https://en.wikipedia.org/wiki/Seven_hills_of_Rome.
Severus, Sulpitius. 1894. Sacred History, Nicene and Post-Nicene Fathers, Second Series. Edited by Philip Schaff, Henry Wace, and Kevin Knight. Translated by Alexander Roberts. Vol. 11. 14 vols. Buffalo, NY: Christian Literature Publishing Co. https://www.newadvent.org/fathers/3505.htm.
Shanks, Hershel. 2022. "The Destruction of Pompeii—God's Revenge?" Biblical Archaeology Society. https://www.biblicalarchaeology.org/daily/ancient-cultures/ancient-near-eastern-world/the-destruction-of-pompeii-gods-revenge/.
"Sibylline Oracles, Book IV." n.d. Holy, Holy, Holy. Accessed December 10, 2022. https://trisagionseraph.tripod.com/Texts/Sibyl4.html.
Simmons, Kurt M. 2010. Revelation Explained: A Contemporary Historical Analysis of the Apocalypse. N.p.: Biblical Publishing.
Smalley, Stephen S. 2012. The Revelation to John: A Commentary on the Greek Text of the Apocalypse. N.p.: InterVarsity Press.
Spirit & Truth. 2013. "The Prophetic Perfect." Spirit & Truth. https://spiritandtruthonline.org/the-prophetic-perfect/?tot=redirect.

Stevens, Edward E., and Michael A. Nichols. 2014. Final Decade Before the End: Jewish and Christian History Just Before the Jewish Revolt. Bradford, Pennsylvania: International Preterist Association.

"Strong's Greek: 1093. γῆ (gé) -- the earth, land." n.d. Bible Hub. Accessed December 9, 2022. https://biblehub.com/greek/1093.htm.

"Strong's Greek: 3195. μέλλω (melló) -- to be about to." n.d. Bible Hub. Accessed December 30, 2022. https://biblehub.com/greek/3195.htm.

"Strong's Greek: 3364. οὐ (ou mé) -- anymore, at all, neither, never." n.d. Bible Hub. Accessed January 25, 2023. https://biblehub.com/greek/3364.htm.

"Strong's Greek: 3588. ὁ, (ho, hé, to) -- the." n.d. Bible Hub. Accessed December 15, 2022. https://biblehub.com/greek/3588.htm.

"Strong's Greek: 360. ἀναλύω (analuó) -- to unloose for departure." n.d. Bible Hub. Accessed December 15, 2022. https://biblehub.com/greek/360.htm.

"Strong's Greek: 4747. στοιχεῖον (stoicheion) -- one of a row, hence a letter (of the alphabet), by ext. the elements (of knowledge)." n.d. Bible Hub. Accessed February 12, 2023. https://biblehub.com/greek/4747.htm.

"Strong's Hebrew: 7307. רוּחַ (ruach) -- breath, wind, spirit." n.d. Bible Hub. Accessed December 12, 2022. https://biblehub.com/hebrew/7307.htm.

Tacitus, Cornelius. 2011. The, complete works of Tacitus, The annals. The history. The life of Cnaeus Julius Agricola. Germany and its, tribes. A dialogue on oratory. Edited by Sara Bryant and Moses Hadas. Translated by Alfred J. Church and William J. Brodribb. Medford, Massachusetts: Perseus Project. http://data.perseus.org/catalog/urn:cts:latinLit:phi1351.phi004.perseus-eng1.

Tertullian. 1885. Apology, From Ante-Nicene Fathers. Edited by Alexander Roberts, James Donaldson, A. C. Coxe., and Kevin Knight. Translated by S. Thelwall. Vol. 3. Buffalo, NY:

Christian Literature Publishing Co. https://www.newadvent.org/fathers/0301.htm.

"Thousands rose from the dead with Jesus on Easter." n.d. Bible Probe. Accessed December 9, 2022. http://www.bibleprobe.com/descent.htm.

Tranquillus, Caius S. 1914. The Life of Nero, The Lives of the Twelve Caesars. Translated by John C. Rolfe. Loeb Classical Library ed. http://penelope.uchicago.edu/Thayer/E/Roman/Texts/Suetonius/12Caesars/Nero*.html.

Tranquillus, Caius S. 1914. The Life of Titus, The Lives of the Twelve Caesars. Translated by John C. Rolfe. Loeb Classical Library ed. https://penelope.uchicago.edu/Thayer/E/Roman/Texts/Suetonius/12Caesars/Titus*.html.

Von Mosheim, Johann L. 2006. Historical Commentaries on the State of Christianity During the First Three Hundred and Twenty-Five Years from the Christian Era, 2 Volumes. Edited by James Murdock. Translated by Robert S. Vidal. (As cited by http://www.ecclesia.org/truth/beast.html) ed. N.p.: Wipf & Stock Publishers.

Westcott, Brooke F. 1903. The Epistle to the Hebrews. Third Edition ed. New York: The Macmillan Company. https://biblicalstudies.org.uk/pdf/e-books/westcott_b-f/hebrews_westcott.pdf.

Wikipedia. 2022. "Flight to Pella." Wikipedia. https://en.wikipedia.org/wiki/Flight_to_Pella.

Williams, Kevin. 2019. "Scientific Evidence Supporting Near-Death Experiences and the Afterlife." Near-Death Experiences and the Afterlife. https://near-death.com/afterlife-evidence/.

World Video Bible School (WVBS). 2015. "Premillennialism: A Deeper Study." YouTube. https://youtu.be/e22iIXj0cVY?t=784.

Yosippon, Sepher. n.d. A Mediaeval History of Ancient Israel. Translated by Steven B. Bowman. N.p.: Excerpts from Chapter 87 "Burning of the Temple" cited in http://fulfilledtheology.ning.com/forum/topics/historical-records-with-some. Accessed Dec. 8, 2022.

Younger, Pliny t. 1900. Letters. Translated by John B. Firth. R.A.B.Mynors' Latin ed. http://www.attalus.org/info/pliny.html.
Zaimov, Stoyan. 2016. "Do Thousands of Near-Death Experiences Prove Heaven Is Real?" Christian Post. https://www.christianpost.com/news/near-death-experiences-prove-heaven-is-real-pastor-john-burke.html.

About the Author

Jon Paul was born and raised in middle Tennessee and is married to his lovely wife, Gabby Miles, who is from Venezuela. They live with their white Siberian Husky, Dakota. Jon Paul is a web designer/developer and likes to blog, study, converse with friends and family, go on walks, play piano, and eat tasty meals. The most important thing in Jon Paul's life is his faith and relationship with Jesus. His hope is to honor the Lord with his research.

You can see his latest work at his blog, Revelations in Grace:

https://revelationsingrace.netlify.app/

Printed in Dunstable, United Kingdom

72126945R00143